Microwave cooking times in this book are approximate. Numerous variables, such as the microwave oven's rated wattage and the starting temperature, shape, amount and depth of food can affect cooking time. Use the cooking times as a guideline and check doneness before adding more time. Lower wattage ovens may consistently require longer cooking times.

FAST FABULOUS MINUTE® RICE

You can serve rice, one of the world's great starches, a number of ways. "Au naturel" is fine—and simple. Or, you can use rice as the starting point for soups, salads, main dishes, main-dish accompaniments, appetizers, or even desserts. This recipe book provides over 100 fast fabulous MINUTE Rice recipes from appetizers to desserts that both you and your family will love.

And MINUTE Rice speeds the preparation of all these dishes. Because it's pre-cooked, MINUTE Rice is ready in just 5 minutes. And it comes out fluffy and tender *every* time—the ideal recipe rice!

So whether it's a special dinner, a family meal, a hearty soup, or a cool summer salad, you'll find the perfect time-saving great-tasting recipe for any and every occasion.

NUTRITIOUS MINUTE® RICE

All-natural MINUTE Rice is 100% USDA grade #1 rice—the highest quality available. We simply precook this long grain rice and then dry it to give you natural perfect rice in 5 minutes.

In addition to being a good source of complex carbohydrate, MINUTE Rice is also enriched with thiamine, niacin and iron. Based on a $2/3$-cup serving (cooked), MINUTE Rice provides

	U.S. RDA Recommended Daily Allowance
Thiamine	10%
Niacin	6%
Iron	6%
Protein	4%

Prepared without butter or salt—which, as the package directions point out, are optional—a $2/3$-cup serving of MINUTE Rice contains only 120 calories and no fat, cholesterol or sodium (ideal for a sodium-restricted diet). How's that for fitting today's lighter, leaner eating style!

VERSATILE MINUTE® RICE

For over 40 years, MINUTE has been the leader in convenient rices. Its quick, easy, foolproof preparation provides light and fluffy rice perfect every time. And it's ideal for recipes. MINUTE Rice soaks up all the natural recipe flavors to enhance any recipe favorite.

Even all by itself, MINUTE Rice is very versatile. Add an ingredient or two in basic preparation, and it takes on a completely new character. Be sure to try these fast fabulous ideas with MINUTE Rice.

- Stir grated lemon, lime or orange rind into the water (1½ teaspoons of rind for 4 servings of rice).

- Add a dash of chili powder, curry, crushed basil leaves or other herb in place of salt.

- Stir in grated or shredded cheese while rice is still hot (¼ cup cheese for 4 servings of rice).

- Add chopped walnuts, peanuts or cashews to rice just before serving (¼ cup nuts for 4 servings of rice).

- Add chopped fresh parsley or chives to prepared rice (2 tablespoons for 4 servings of rice).

- Add slivered almonds and raisins to prepared rice (2 tablespoons *each* for 4 servings of rice).

- Substitute your favorite bouillon or broth for all or part of the water.

- For quick and easy super rice, prepare any cream-style soup according to can directions. Then, fill the can with MINUTE Rice and add to boiling soup. Stir, cover, remove from heat, and let stand 10 minutes. Serve hot.

- For each serving, add one slice (¾ oz. or 1 oz.) of process American cheese to boiling water. After cheese melts, stir in rice. Cover, remove from heat, and let stand 10 minutes. For creamier rice, use half milk and half water.

- See side of package for "Amounts of Rice and Water." Use the same amount of spaghetti sauce as water and bring both to a boil. Stir in rice. Cover, remove from heat, and let stand 10 minutes. Sprinkle with grated Parmesan cheese, if desired.

MOST REQUESTED MINUTE® RICE RECIPES

Everyone has their own favorite MINUTE Rice recipe. Here are some of the all-time favorites:

As great as the old classics are, be sure to try the countless fast fabulous dishes brought to you by MINUTE. Bon Appetit!

Appetizers and Soups

LOUISIANA TOMATO-RICE GUMBO

     1 whole boned chicken breast, cut into pieces
     3 tablespoons butter or margarine
 1/2 cup chopped onion
 1/2 cup chopped green pepper
 1/2 cup chopped celery
     1 garlic clove, minced
     1 package (10 oz.) frozen okra, thawed and sliced*
     1 can (16 oz.) crushed tomatoes
     1 can (13³/₄ oz.) ready-to-serve chicken broth
     1 teaspoon salt
     1 small bay leaf
 1/2 teaspoon sugar
 1/8 teaspoon thyme leaves
        Dash of pepper
 1/2 pound shrimp, cleaned
 1¹/₃ cups MINUTE® Rice

Cook and stir chicken in hot butter in large skillet until lightly browned. Stir in onion, green pepper, celery and garlic; cook until tender.

Add okra, tomatoes, broth and seasonings. Bring to a boil. Reduce heat; cover and simmer 5 minutes, stirring occasionally. Add shrimp and cook 5 minutes. Remove bay leaf. Stir in rice. Cover; remove from heat. Let stand 5 minutes. Makes 6 servings.

*You may use 1 package (10 oz.) BIRDS EYE® Cut Green Beans for the frozen okra.

LOUISIANA TOMATO-RICE GUMBO

COUNTRY CHICKEN-VEGETABLE SOUP

COUNTRY CHICKEN-VEGETABLE SOUP

2 cans (13³/₄ oz. each) ready-to-serve chicken broth
¹/₂ teaspoon salt
¹/₂ teaspoon dried tarragon leaves
1 package (16 oz.) BIRDS EYE® FARM FRESH Mixtures, any variety
2 cups diced cooked chicken
¹/₂ cup MINUTE® Rice

Combine all ingredients except rice in large saucepan. Bring to a boil. Reduce heat; simmer 2 minutes. Stir in rice. Cover; remove from heat. Let stand 5 minutes. Makes 6 servings.

STUFFED GRAPE LEAVES

1/2 **pound ground beef**
1 **medium onion, chopped**
  Greek Salad Dressing (recipe follows)
3/4 **cup MINUTE® Rice**
1/4 **cup chopped parsley**
1/4 **teaspoon salt**
20 **canned grape leaves**

Brown beef with onion in medium skillet. Stir in 1/4 cup of the dressing, the rice, parsley and salt. With shiny surface of leaf down, place 1 tablespoon of the meat mixture in center of each leaf. Fold edges of leaf toward center and roll up. Place in large skillet. Pour remaining 3/4 cup dressing over stuffed leaves and simmer over low heat until liquid is absorbed, about 5 minutes. Cover and chill. Makes 20 servings.

GREEK SALAD DRESSING

3 **tablespoons lemon juice**
3 **tablespoons water**
1 **envelope GOOD SEASONS® Lemon and Herbs or Italian**
  Salad Dressing Mix
2/3 **cup olive oil**
3 **tablespoons feta cheese, crumbled (optional)**
1/2 **teaspoon dried oregano leaves**

Combine lemon juice, water and salad dressing mix in cruet or jar. Shake well. Add olive oil, feta cheese and oregano. Shake well. Makes 1 cup.

PEASE PORRIDGE HOT

4 **slices bacon**
3/4 **cup chopped onions**
2 **cans (11 1/4 oz. each) condensed green pea soup**
3 **cans (4 cups) water**
1 1/3 **cups MINUTE® Rice**
3/4 **teaspoon salt**

Cook bacon in large saucepan until crisp. Remove bacon; drain on absorbent paper and crumble. Reserve 2 tablespoons drippings. Cook and stir onions in reserved drippings until tender and lightly browned. Add soup; then gradually mix in water. Bring to a full boil. Add rice, salt and bacon. Cover; remove from heat. Let stand 5 minutes. Makes 8 servings.

COCKALEEKIE

4 cans (13³/₄ oz. each) ready-to-serve chicken broth
1 cup water
6 leeks, split and cut into 1-inch pieces*
1¹/₂ to 2 teaspoons salt
¹/₈ teaspoon pepper
1 cup MINUTE® Rice
1 cup thin strips cooked chicken
2 tablespoons minced parsley

Combine broth, water, leeks, salt and pepper in large saucepan. Bring to a boil. Reduce heat; simmer 15 minutes or until leeks are just tender. Add rice and chicken. Cover; remove from heat. Let stand 5 minutes. Sprinkle with parsley. Makes 8 servings.

*You may use 2 bunches scallions, cut into ¹/₂-inch pieces for the leeks.

TUNA PUFFS

1¹/₃ cups water
¹/₂ teaspoon salt
1¹/₃ cups MINUTE® Rice
1 can (10³/₄ oz.) condensed cream of mushroom soup
1 can (6¹/₂ oz.) tuna, drained and finely flaked
1 egg
2 tablespoons chopped parsley
2 tablespoons finely chopped onion
2 teaspoons lemon juice
¹/₄ teaspoon Worcestershire sauce
Dash of pepper
Dry bread crumbs (about ¹/₂ cup)
Oil for frying

Bring water and salt to a full boil in medium saucepan. Stir in rice. Cover; remove from heat. Let stand 5 minutes. Meanwhile, mix together soup, tuna, egg, parsley, onion, lemon juice, Worcestershire sauce and pepper in medium bowl. Then add rice and mix thoroughly. Cover and chill at least 1 hour.

Shape chilled mixture into oblong or round croquettes, using about 1 tablespoon of the mixture. Roll in bread crumbs. Fry in ¹/₂ inch hot (400°) oil, turning to brown both sides. Serve appetizer puff with a seafood cocktail sauce, if desired. Makes about 56 appetizers.

COCKALEEKIE

TOMATO, CHICKEN AND MUSHROOM SOUP

1/4 **pound mushrooms, sliced***
1 **tablespoon butter or margarine**
2 **cans (13³/₄ oz. each) ready-to-serve chicken broth**
2 **cups diced cooked chicken**
1 **can (14¹/₂ oz.) whole tomatoes**
1 **can (8 oz.) tomato sauce**
1 **carrot, thinly sliced**
1 **envelope GOOD SEASONS® Italian Salad Dressing Mix**
3/4 **cup MINUTE® Rice**

Cook and stir mushrooms in hot butter in large saucepan. Gradually stir in broth; then add chicken, tomatoes, tomato sauce, carrot and salad dressing mix. Bring to a boil. Reduce heat; cover and simmer 10 minutes. Stir in rice. Cover; remove from heat. Let stand 5 minutes. Makes 8 servings.

*You may use 1 jar (4.5 oz.) drained sliced mushrooms for the fresh mushrooms.

TOMATO, CHICKEN AND MUSHROOM SOUP

QUICK AND EASY VEGETABLE-RICE SOUP

    2 cans (13³/₄ oz. each) ready-to-serve chicken broth
    1 package (16 oz.) BIRDS EYE® FARM FRESH Mixtures, any
        variety
    2 tablespoons chopped scallions
    2 tablespoons lemon juice
    ¹/₂ teaspoon ground nutmeg
    ¹/₄ cup MINUTE® Rice

Bring broth to a boil in large saucepan. Add remaining ingredients, except rice.
Reduce heat; simmer 4 minutes. Stir in rice. Cover; remove from heat. Let stand
5 minutes. Makes 4 servings.

CREAMY NEW ENGLAND CHOWDER

    1 can (10³/₄ oz.) condensed cream of celery soup
    2 cups water
    1 bottle (8 oz.) clam juice
    1 can (7¹/₂ oz.) minced clams
    ³/₄ cup milk or light cream
    1 tablespoon butter or margarine
    1 tablespoon chopped parsley
    1 teaspoon salt
    1 cup MINUTE® Rice
    2 teaspoons lemon juice

Mix soup with water and clam juice in large saucepan. Add clams, milk, butter,
parsley and salt. Bring to a boil. Reduce heat; simmer 5 minutes. Stir in rice and
lemon juice. Cover; remove from heat. Let stand 5 minutes. Garnish with
additional chopped parsley, if desired. Makes 6 servings.

SPINACH-RICE SOUP

    1 can (13³/₄ oz.) ready-to-serve chicken broth
    1 package (11 oz.) BIRDS EYE® Creamed Spinach, thawed
    ¹/₄ cup MINUTE® Rice
        Dash of pepper
        Dash of ground nutmeg

Bring broth and spinach to a full boil in medium saucepan. Stir in rice. Cover;
remove from heat. Let stand 5 minutes. Season with pepper and nutmeg. Makes
3 servings.

Note: Recipe may be doubled.

TOP: OLE DELAWARE CRAB-RICE CAKES
BOTTOM: ITALIAN STUFFED MUSHROOMS

ITALIAN STUFFED MUSHROOMS

   1/4 **pound Italian or bulk pork sausage**
   1 **cup chopped onions**
   1 **pound (about 12) large mushrooms**
   3/4 **cup water**
   1 **tablespoon finely chopped parsley**
   1/2 **teaspoon salt**
   1/8 **teaspoon pepper**
   3/4 **cup MINUTE® Rice**
   3/4 **cup mayonnaise**
   1/2 **cup grated Parmesan cheese**

continued

Brown sausage with onions in medium skillet, breaking up meat with fork. Meanwhile, remove stems from mushrooms. Chop stems very fine and add to meat mixture; cook until lightly browned.

Add water, parsley, salt and pepper. Bring to a full boil. Stir in rice. Cover; remove from heat. Let stand 5 minutes.

Mix mayonnaise and cheese in small bowl. Stir 1/2 cup of the mayonnaise mixture into rice mixture. Spoon into mushroom caps. Place in shallow baking dish. Top with remaining mayonnaise mixture. Bake at 400° about 15 minutes or until browned and puffy. Makes about 12 appetizers.

OLE DELAWARE CRAB-RICE CAKES

>   3/4 **cup mayonnaise**
>   3/4 **cup sour cream**
>   1 **tablespoon prepared horseradish**
>   1 **envelope GOOD SEASONS® Lemon and Herbs or Italian**
>   **Salad Dressing Mix**
>   1 **cup water**
>   1/2 **teaspoon salt**
>   **Dash of pepper**
>   1 **cup MINUTE® Rice**
>   1/2 **cup crabmeat or imitation crabmeat**
>   2 **eggs, well beaten**
>   2 **tablespoons all-purpose flour**
>   1 **tablespoon chopped onion**
>   3 **tablespoons butter or margarine**

Mix together mayonnaise, sour cream, horseradish and salad dressing mix in small bowl. Set aside 1/2 cup; cover and chill remaining dressing.

Bring water, salt and pepper to a full boil. Stir in rice. Cover; remove from heat. Let stand 5 minutes. Mix in crabmeat, eggs, flour, onion and the reserved 1/2 cup dressing.

Melt butter in large skillet. Drop rice mixture by tablespoonfuls into skillet and fry, turning to brown both sides. Serve as an appetizer with the remaining chilled dressing. Makes 40 cakes.

HEARTY MEATBALL SOUP

1/2 **pound ground beef**
1/2 **pound bulk pork sausage**
1 **egg**
1 1/2 **teaspoons salt**
1/8 **teaspoon pepper (optional)**
4 **cups water**
1 **envelope (4-serving size) onion soup mix**
1 **can (15 1/4 oz.) red kidney beans, drained**
1 **can (14 1/2 oz.) stewed tomatoes**
1 **cup diced carrots**
1 **cup MINUTE® Rice**
2 **tablespoons chopped parsley**

Mix ground beef, sausage, egg, salt and pepper thoroughly in medium bowl. Shape into tiny balls. (Brown meatballs in skillet, if desired.)

Bring water to a boil in large saucepan; stir in soup mix. Reduce heat; cover and simmer 10 minutes. Add meatballs, kidney beans, tomatoes and carrots; simmer 15 minutes longer. Stir in rice. Cover; remove from heat. Let stand 5 minutes. Add parsley. Makes 8 servings.

EASY TOMATO-CHEESE BISQUE

1 **can (11 oz.) condensed cheddar cheese soup**
2 **cups water**
1 **cup tomato juice**
1 **tablespoon butter or margarine**
1 **tablespoon chopped chives (optional)**
1/2 **teaspoon salt**
1/2 **teaspoon sugar**
1/2 **teaspoon dry mustard**
1/2 **teaspoon Worcestershire sauce**
1 **cup MINUTE® Rice**
3/4 **cup milk, light cream or evaporated milk**

Mix soup with water and tomato juice in large saucepan. Add butter, chives and seasonings. Bring to a full boil. Stir in rice and milk. Reduce heat; cover and simmer 10 minutes, stirring occasionally. Garnish with additional chopped chives or popcorn, if desired. Makes 5 servings.

HEARTY MEATBALL SOUP

FESTIVE COCKTAIL MEATBALLS

1½ pounds ground beef
1 cup MINUTE® Rice
1 can (8 oz.) crushed pineapple in juice
½ cup finely shredded carrot
⅓ cup chopped onion
1 egg, slightly beaten
1 teaspoon ground ginger
1 bottle (8 oz.) prepared French dressing
2 tablespoons soy sauce

Mix ground beef, rice, pineapple, carrot, onion, egg and ginger in medium bowl. Form into 1-inch meatballs. Place on greased baking sheets. Bake at 400° for 15 minutes or until browned.

Meanwhile, mix together dressing and soy sauce. Serve meatballs with dressing mixture. Makes 50 to 60 meatballs.

CORN CHOWDER

2 slices bacon
1 medium onion, chopped
1 stalk celery, sliced
4 teaspoons all-purpose flour
3 cups milk
1 cup water
1 package (10 oz.) BIRDS EYE® Sweet Corn
1 chicken bouillon cube
1 teaspoon salt
¼ teaspoon pepper
1 cup MINUTE® Rice
1 tablespoon chopped parsley

Cook bacon in large saucepan until crisp. Remove bacon; drain on absorbent paper. Crumble and set aside.

Cook and stir onion and celery in bacon drippings until tender; stir in flour. Add milk, water, corn, bouillon cube, salt and pepper. Bring to a boil. Reduce heat; simmer 5 minutes. Stir in rice, bacon and parsley. Cover; remove from heat. Let stand 5 minutes. Makes 6 servings.

FESTIVE COCKTAIL MEATBALLS

Salads

SPICY CAJUN RICE SALAD

        2 cups water
     ³/₄ teaspoon salt
        2 cups MINUTE® Rice
     ¹/₂ cup prepared GOOD SEASONS® Italian or Zesty Italian
           Salad Dressing
    1¹/₂ teaspoons hot pepper sauce
        2 teaspoons prepared hot spicy mustard
        2 hard-cooked eggs, chopped
     ¹/₂ cup diced celery
     ¹/₂ cup toasted pecans, cut into pieces
     ¹/₄ cup sliced scallions
     ¹/₄ cup sliced stuffed green olives
     ¹/₄ cup chopped parsley
     ¹/₄ cup sweet pickle relish
        1 tablespoon diced dill pickle

Bring water and salt to a full boil in medium saucepan. Stir in rice. Cover;
remove from heat. Let stand 5 minutes. Fluff with fork. Cool.

Combine salad dressing, pepper sauce and mustard in small bowl; blend well.
Combine rice with remaining ingredients in large bowl. Spoon dressing mixture
over salad, tossing to coat. Cover and chill. Makes 6 servings.

SPICY CAJUN RICE SALAD

GARDEN CHICKEN SALAD

GARDEN CHICKEN SALAD

- 1/3 cup mayonnaise
- 1/3 cup sour cream
- 1/4 cup cold water
- 2 tablespoons prepared mustard
- 1 teaspoon sugar
- 1 teaspoon dried oregano leaves
- 1 teaspoon garlic powder
- 1 teaspoon salt
- 1/4 teaspoon pepper
- 1/4 cup finely chopped parsley
- 2 teaspoons vinegar
- 1 1/2 cups boiling water
- 1 1/2 cups MINUTE® Rice
- 1 small onion, sliced or diced
- 1 1/2 cups diced cooked chicken or turkey
- 1 package (16 oz.) BIRDS EYE® Broccoli Cuts, thawed and drained
- 1/2 cup sliced celery
- 8 cherry tomatoes, halved
  Lettuce leaves

continued

To make dressing, mix mayonnaise, sour cream, cold water, mustard, sugar, oregano, garlic powder, salt, pepper, parsley and vinegar in small bowl.

Pour boiling water over rice and onion in 2-quart bowl. Cover and let stand 5 minutes. Stir in dressing. Add chicken, broccoli, celery and tomatoes, mixing lightly. Spoon into lettuce-lined bowl or platter. Serve at once or cover and chill. Store any leftover salad in refrigerator. Makes 4 servings.

To make ahead: Combine all ingredients for dressing in bowl; blend well. Cover and chill. Prepare rice as directed. Add all ingredients except dressing and tomatoes. Cover and chill. Just before serving, toss dressing with rice mixture and garnish with tomatoes.

WALDORF RICE SALAD

1¹/₂ cups boiling water
1¹/₂ cups MINUTE® Rice
 ¹/₂ cup chilled prepared GOOD SEASONS® Italian Salad
       Dressing
  2 cups diced unpeeled red apples
 ¹/₂ cup slivered Swiss cheese
 ¹/₂ cup sliced celery
 ¹/₂ cup chopped walnuts
 ¹/₄ cup mayonnaise
 ¹/₄ cup plain yogurt
     Lettuce leaves

Pour boiling water over rice in 2-quart bowl. Cover and let stand 5 minutes. Stir in salad dressing. Then stir in apples, cheese, celery, walnuts, mayonnaise and yogurt, mixing lightly. Spoon into lettuce-lined bowl or platter. Garnish with apple slices, if desired. Serve at once or cover and chill. Makes 4 servings.

ANTIPASTO SALAD

1¹/₃ cups water
 ¹/₂ teaspoon salt
1¹/₃ cups MINUTE® Rice
  1 cup Genoa salami, diced
  1 cup Provolone cheese, cut into ¹/₂-inch pieces
 ¹/₄ cup pitted ripe olives
 ¹/₄ cup roasted red pepper strips
 ¹/₂ cup prepared GOOD SEASONS® Italian Salad Dressing

Bring water and salt to a full boil in medium saucepan. Stir in rice. Cover; remove from heat. Let stand until cool. Mix with remaining ingredients. Serve at once or cover and chill. Makes 4 servings.

THREE BEAN RICE SALAD

    1 can (16 oz.) cut wax beans, drained
    1 can (16 oz.) French-style green beans, drained
    1 can (8³/₄ oz.) red kidney beans, drained
    ¹/₂ cup prepared GOOD SEASONS® Italian Salad Dressing
    ¹/₄ cup thinly sliced onion rings
    1 teaspoon salt
    ¹/₈ teaspoon pepper
    1¹/₂ cups water
    1¹/₂ cups MINUTE® Rice

Mix beans, salad dressing, onion, ¹/₂ teaspoon of the salt and the pepper in large bowl; set aside to allow flavors to blend.

Meanwhile, bring water and remaining ¹/₂ teaspoon salt to a full boil in medium saucepan. Stir in rice. Cover; remove from heat. Let stand 5 minutes. Fold rice into bean mixture. Cover and chill thoroughly. Serve on lettuce. Makes 6 servings.

SAVORY VEGETABLE SALAD

    1¹/₂ cups water
    1 teaspoon salt
    1¹/₂ cups MINUTE® Rice
    ¹/₄ cup prepared French dressing
    ³/₄ cup mayonnaise
    1 tablespoon finely chopped onion
    1 tablespoon lemon juice
    ³/₄ teaspoon curry powder
    ¹/₂ teaspoon dry mustard
    ¹/₈ teaspoon pepper
    1 package (10 oz.) BIRDS EYE® Green Peas or Mixed
        Vegetables, thawed
    1 cup diced celery

Bring water and ¹/₂ teaspoon of the salt to a full boil in medium saucepan. Stir in rice. Cover; remove from heat. Let stand 5 minutes. Add French dressing, mixing lightly with fork; cool.

Blend mayonnaise, onion, lemon juice, curry powder, remaining ¹/₂ teaspoon salt, the mustard and pepper in large bowl. Add peas and celery; add rice and mix lightly with fork. Cover and chill at least 1 hour. Serve on salad greens with sliced ham, if desired. Store any leftover salad in refrigerator. Makes 6 servings.

THREE BEAN RICE SALAD

MEXICALE HOT TACO SALAD

1 pound ground beef
1 small green pepper, cut into thin strips
1 onion, chopped
1 jar (12 oz.) medium salsa
1 can (8 oz.) tomato sauce
1 chicken bouillon cube
1¹/₂ cups MINUTE® Rice
   Shredded iceberg lettuce
   Tomato wedges
   Sour cream
   Shredded cheddar cheese
   Sliced pitted ripe olives
   Tortilla chips

Brown beef, pepper and onion in large skillet. Add salsa, tomato sauce and bouillon cube. Bring to a full boil. Stir in rice. Cover; remove from heat. Let stand 5 minutes. Fluff with fork.

Serve with lettuce, tomatoes, sour cream, shredded cheese, olives and tortilla chips. Makes 4 servings.

ZESTY CHICKEN TACO RICE SALAD

1 pound boned chicken breasts, cut into strips
2 tablespoons oil
1 can (13³/₄ oz.) ready-to-serve chicken broth
1 can (8 oz.) tomato sauce
1 package taco seasoning mix
1 can (12 oz.) corn, drained
1 medium red or green pepper (or a combination), cut into
   thin strips
1¹/₂ cups MINUTE® Rice
¹/₂ cup (2 oz.) shredded cheddar cheese
   Tortilla chips

Cook and stir chicken in hot oil in large skillet until lightly browned. Add broth, tomato sauce and seasoning mix. Bring to a boil. Reduce heat; cover and simmer 5 minutes. Add corn and red pepper. Bring to a full boil. Stir in rice. Cover; remove from heat. Let stand 5 minutes. Fluff with fork. Serve with cheese and tortilla chips. Makes 4 servings.

TOP: MEXICALE HOT TACO SALAD
BOTTOM: ZESTY CHICKEN TACO RICE SALAD

VERY VERSATILE RICE SALAD

1½ cups water
½ teaspoon salt
1½ cups MINUTE® Rice
1¾ cups diced canned or cooked meat, seafood or poultry
1 cup canned or cooked vegetables
½ cup condiments
¾ cup mayonnaise
Seasonings to taste

Bring water and salt to a full boil in medium saucepan. Stir in rice. Cover; remove from heat. Let stand 5 minutes. Fluff with fork. Cool to room temperature. Combine meat, vegetables and condiments in medium bowl. Fold in mayonnaise and seasonings, blending well. Add rice and mix lightly with fork. Cover and chill about 1 hour. Makes 4 servings.

Suggested Meats: bacon, beef or dried beef, cold cuts or luncheon meat, frankfurters, ham, lamb, pork, tongue or veal.

Suggested Seafood: cod, crab, flounder, haddock, halibut, lobster, ocean perch, salmon, sole, shrimp, whiting or tuna.

Suggested Poultry: chicken, duck or turkey.

Suggested Vegetables: artichoke hearts, corn, green beans, lima beans, mixed vegetables, peas, peas and carrots or succotash.

Suggested Condiments: celery, cheese, hard-cooked eggs, mushrooms, nuts, olives, green pepper, pickles or pimiento.

Suggested Seasonings: capers, catsup, chili sauce, chives, curry powder, garlic, fresh or dried herbs, lemon juice, mustard, onion or parsley.

RICE AND CORN SALAD

1½ cups water
1 teaspoon salt
1½ cups MINUTE® Rice
1 package (10 oz.) BIRDS EYE® Sweet Corn, thawed
½ cup thinly sliced celery
¼ cup chopped onion
½ cup mayonnaise
2 tablespoons chopped parsley (optional)
⅛ teaspoon pepper

Bring water and salt to a full boil in medium saucepan. Stir in rice. Cover; remove from heat. Let stand 5 minutes. Fluff with fork. Cover and chill thoroughly. Add remaining ingredients; mix lightly. Serve at once or cover and chill. Store any leftover salad in refrigerator. Makes 4 servings.

TUNA-VEGETABLE SALAD

1½ **cups water**
1 **package (10 oz.) BIRDS EYE® Green Peas**
1 **medium carrot, thinly sliced**
2 **tablespoons chopped onion**
½ **teaspoon salt**
⅛ **teaspoon pepper**
1½ **cups MINUTE® Rice**
1 **can (6½ oz.) water-packed tuna, drained and flaked**
1 **cup mayonnaise**
½ **cup chopped dill pickle**
¼ **cup milk**

Bring water, peas, carrot, onion, salt and pepper to a full boil in medium saucepan. Stir in rice. Cover; remove from heat. Let stand 5 minutes. Fluff with fork. Cover and chill.

Just before serving, gently stir in tuna, mayonnaise, pickle and milk. If desired, serve on crisp salad greens and garnish. Makes 6 servings.

TUNA-VEGETABLE SALAD

FANTASTIC LAYERED SALAD

1¹/₃ cups water
¹/₂ teaspoon salt
1¹/₃ cups MINUTE® Rice
3¹/₂ cups shredded iceberg lettuce (1 head)
1 small red onion, thinly sliced
1 package (10 oz.) BIRDS EYE® Green Peas, thawed
1 can (15¹/₄ oz.) red kidney beans, drained
1 cup prepared GOOD SEASONS® Italian or Cheese Italian
  Salad Dressing

Bring water and salt to a full boil in medium saucepan. Stir in rice. Cover; remove from heat. Let stand 5 minutes. Fluff with fork; cool.

Place 1¹/₂ cups of the lettuce in 2-quart straight-sided bowl. Add half of the onion and top with half of the rice. Add a layer of peas. Repeat lettuce, onion and rice layers. Top with kidney beans and add remaining lettuce. Cover and chill. About 1 hour before serving, pour dressing evenly over salad and cover and chill. Store any leftover salad in refrigerator. Makes 8 servings.

GREEK-STYLE RICE SALAD

1¹/₂ cups water
1 envelope GOOD SEASONS® Lemon and Herbs Salad
  Dressing Mix
1¹/₂ cups MINUTE® Rice
3 tablespoons oil
1 tablespoon vinegar
1 teaspoon dried dill weed or 1 tablespoon chopped
  fresh dill
1 large tomato, cut into thin wedges
1 medium cucumber, seeded and thinly sliced
4 ounces feta cheese, cubed

Bring water and salad dressing mix to a full boil in medium saucepan. Stir in rice. Cover; remove from heat. Let stand 5 minutes. Fluff with fork.

Meanwhile, blend oil, vinegar and dill weed in large bowl. Gently stir in rice, tomato, cucumber and feta cheese to coat well. Serve at room temperature. Makes 4 servings.

FANTASTIC LAYERED SALAD

Meat Entrees

DELI-IN-A-SKILLET

1/2 pound corned beef, cooked and cut into pieces*
1 can (14 oz.) sauerkraut
1 1/2 cups water
1 1/2 cups MINUTE® Rice
1/2 cup prepared Thousand Island dressing
3 ounces Swiss cheese, cut into strips

Mix corned beef, sauerkraut and water in large skillet. Bring to a full boil. Stir in rice. Pour dressing over rice and top with cheese. Cover; remove from heat. Let stand 5 minutes. Makes 4 servings.

*You may use Knockwurst or other luncheon meat cut into pieces for the corned beef.

HOME-STYLE CHILI WITH RICE

1 pound ground beef
1 can (15 1/4 oz.) kidney beans, drained
1 can (13 3/4 oz.) ready-to-serve beef broth
1 can (8 oz.) tomato sauce
1 package chili seasoning mix
1 1/2 cups MINUTE® Rice
1 small green pepper, chopped (1 cup)
1 can (4 oz.) chopped peeled green mild chilies, drained

Brown beef in large skillet. Add kidney beans, broth, tomato sauce and chili seasoning mix. Bring to a boil. Reduce heat; cover and simmer 5 minutes, stirring occasionally. Bring to a full boil. Stir in rice, green pepper and chilies. Cover; remove from heat. Let stand 5 minutes. Fluff with fork. Makes 4 servings.

DELI-IN-A-SKILLET

BEEF ITALIANO

BEEF ITALIANO

- ³/₄ **pound ground beef**
- 1 **small red pepper, cubed**
- 1 **small green pepper, cubed**
- 1 **medium onion, cut into wedges**
- 1 **can (14¹/₂ oz.) whole tomatoes**
- 1 **cup beef broth**
- 1¹/₂ **teaspoons salt**
- 1 **teaspoon dried basil leaves**
- ¹/₂ to ³/₄ **teaspoon pepper**
- ¹/₂ **teaspoon dried oregano leaves**
- 1¹/₂ **cups MINUTE® Rice**

Brown beef, peppers and onion in large skillet. Add tomatoes, broth and seasonings. Bring to a full boil, breaking up tomatoes with edge of spoon. Stir in rice. Cover; remove from heat. Let stand 5 minutes. Fluff with fork. Makes 4 servings.

SKILLET BEEF ENCHILADA

1 pound ground beef
1 large onion, chopped
1 can (15¼ oz.) kidney beans, drained
1 can (13¾ oz.) ready-to-serve chicken broth
1 package taco mix
1 can (8 oz.) corn, drained
1½ cups MINUTE® Rice
½ cup sour cream
8 flour tortillas, steamed

Brown beef with onion in large skillet, about 5 minutes. Add beans, broth, taco mix and corn. Bring to a full boil. Reduce heat; simmer 5 minutes. Stir in rice. Cover; remove from heat. Let stand 5 minutes. Stir in sour cream. Serve with tortillas. Makes 4 servings.

MICROWAVE DIRECTIONS: Decrease broth to 1¼ cups. Combine beef and onion in 12×7½-inch microwavable dish. Cover with plastic wrap and cook at HIGH 3 minutes. Stir; breaking beef into pieces. Add beans, broth, taco mix, corn and rice. Cover and cook at HIGH 4 minutes. Stir; cover and cook at HIGH 3 to 4 minutes longer. Let stand 5 minutes. Stir in sour cream. Serve with tortillas. Makes 4 servings.

CURRIED BEEF AND RICE

¾ pound London broil, cut into thin strips*
1 tablespoon oil
1 cup sliced onions
1 can (13¾ oz.) ready-to-serve chicken broth
1¼ teaspoons curry powder
1½ cups MINUTE® Rice
1 large tart apple, cored and diced
1 tablespoon finely chopped parsley
2 tablespoons chopped salted peanuts

Brown beef in hot oil in large skillet. Add onions while browning beef and cook until tender. Add broth and curry powder. Bring to a boil. Stir in rice and apple. Cover; remove from heat. Let stand 5 minutes. Fluff with fork; then sprinkle with parsley and peanuts. Makes 4 servings.

*You may use ¾ pound boned chicken breasts, cut into thin strips for the London broil.

VERSATILE SUPER SUPPER RICE

2 cups water
2 cups diced cooked meat or poultry
1 can (10 3/4 oz.) cream-style condensed soup
1 package (16 oz.) BIRDS EYE® FARM FRESH Mixtures, any
variety
Seasonings to taste*
2 cups MINUTE® Rice
Topping**

Mix together all ingredients, except rice and topping, in large skillet. Bring to a boil. Reduce heat; simmer 2 minutes. Stir in rice. Cover; remove from heat. Let stand 5 minutes. Fluff with fork. Sprinkle with topping. Makes 6 servings.

MICROWAVE DIRECTIONS: Mix together all ingredients, except topping, in 2-quart microwavable dish. Cover and cook at HIGH 8 minutes. Stir; cover and cook at HIGH 7 minutes longer. Stir and sprinkle with topping. Makes 6 servings.

*Suggested Seasonings: 1 package taco seasoning mix, 1 can (4 oz.) drained chopped peeled green chilies, salt and pepper, 1 teaspoon of your favorite herb, soy sauce, Worcestershire sauce or dash of hot pepper sauce.

**Suggested Toppings: Crushed corn chips, crushed tortilla chips, shredded cheese, sliced pitted green or ripe olives, 1 can (2.8 oz.) French fried onions, 1 cup chow mein noodles, chopped toasted walnuts or almonds or chopped scallions.

Ground Beef Variation: Brown 1 pound ground beef in large skillet. Use with Nacho cheese or cheddar cheese soup; broccoli, corn and red peppers vegetable mixture; and 1 package taco seasoning mix. Sprinkle with 1/2 cup shredded cheddar cheese or crushed tortilla chips.

For microwave cooking, cook beef in 2-quart microwavable dish at HIGH 2 1/2 minutes. Stir to break up and cook at HIGH 2 1/2 minutes longer. Drain fat. Stir in remaining ingredients except topping. Proceed as directed in Microwave Directions.

Tuna Variation: Use 2 cans (6 1/2 oz. each) tuna, drained and flaked, with cream of mushroom soup; broccoli, green beans, pearl onions and red peppers vegetable mixture; and 1/2 teaspoon salt and 1/8 teaspoon pepper. Sprinkle with 1 can (2.8 oz.) French fried onions.

Chicken or Turkey Variation: Use 2 cups diced cooked chicken or turkey breast with cream of chicken soup; broccoli, red peppers, bamboo shoots and mushroom vegetable mixture; 2 tablespoons soy sauce; 1 tablespoon dry sherry; and 1/4 teaspoon ground ginger. Sprinkle with 1 cup fried noodles.

VERSATILE SUPER SUPPER RICE
(GROUND BEEF VARIATION)

SWEET AND SOUR PORK

2 tablespoons all-purpose flour
1/2 teaspoon salt
1 pound pork tenderloin, cut into 1-inch cubes*
1 tablespoon oil
1 large green pepper, cut into strips
1 can (151/4 oz.) pineapple chunks in heavy syrup
11/2 cups water
2 tablespoons sugar
1 tablespoon cornstarch
1 tablespoon vinegar
11/2 cups MINUTE® Rice

Mix flour and salt in shallow dish. Coat pork cubes with flour mixture. Brown pork well in hot oil over medium heat in large skillet. Continue cooking 10 minutes, stirring occasionally. Always cook pork thoroughly. Add green pepper, pineapple and water. Mix sugar, cornstarch and vinegar in small cup; stir into skillet. Cook and stir until mixture thickens and comes to a full boil. Stir in rice. Cover; remove from heat. Let stand 5 minutes. Fluff with fork. Makes 4 servings.

*You may use 11/4 pounds pork shoulder or butt, trimmed and cut into 1-inch cubes.

SHANGHAI BEEF

1 pound round steak, cut into thin strips
2 tablespoons oil
3 or 4 tablespoons soy sauce
2 tablespoons cornstarch
11/2 cups beef broth
1 can (8 oz.) sliced water chestnuts, drained
1 medium red pepper, coarsely chopped
5 scallions, cut diagonally into 1-inch pieces
1/4 teaspoon pepper
11/2 cups MINUTE® Rice

Brown beef in hot oil in large skillet, about 5 minutes. Mix soy sauce and cornstarch in small cup; stir into beef. Add broth, water chestnuts, red pepper, scallions and pepper. Cook and stir until mixture thickens and comes to a full boil. Stir in rice. Cover; remove from heat. Let stand 5 minutes. Fluff with fork. Makes 4 servings.

MICROWAVE DIRECTIONS: Omit oil. Use 3 tablespoons soy sauce. Mix soy sauce and cornstarch in small cup; stir into remaining ingredients in 2-quart microwavable dish. Cover and cook at HIGH 5 minutes. Stir; cover and cook at HIGH 5 to 6 minutes longer. Fluff with fork. Makes 4 servings.

CLASSIC BEEF STROGANOFF

- ³/₄ **pound sirloin or flank steak, cut into thin strips**
- 2 **tablespoons oil**
- 2 **cups sliced mushrooms**
- 1 **medium onion, sliced**
- 1 **can (13³/₄ oz.) ready-to-serve beef broth**
- 1 **tablespoon Worcestershire sauce**
- ¹/₂ **teaspoon paprika**
- 1¹/₂ **cups MINUTE® Rice**
- ¹/₂ **cup sour cream**
- ¹/₃ **cup catsup or tomato paste**
- 8 **cherry tomatoes, halved**

Brown beef in hot oil in large skillet. Add mushrooms and onion. Cook and stir about 5 minutes. Add broth, Worcestershire sauce and paprika; bring to a full boil. Stir in rice. Cover; remove from heat. Let stand 5 minutes. Stir in sour cream, catsup and cherry tomatoes. Garnish as desired. Makes 4 servings.

MICROWAVE DIRECTIONS: Decrease oil to 1 tablespoon and broth to 1 cup. Place oil in microwavable dish. Stir in beef, mushrooms and onion. Cover and cook at HIGH 2 minutes. Stir; cover and cook at HIGH 2 to 3 minutes longer. Stir in broth, Worcestershire sauce, paprika, rice and catsup. Cover and cook at HIGH 4 minutes. Stir; cover and cook at HIGH 2 to 3 minutes longer. Let stand 5 minutes. Stir in sour cream and tomatoes. Garnish as desired. Makes 4 servings.

CLASSIC BEEF
STROGANOFF

QUICK AND EASY SPANISH RICE AND BEEF

- ³/₄ **pound ground beef**
- 1 **can (14¹/₂ oz.) stewed tomatoes**
- 1 **cup water**
- 1 **package (10 oz.) BIRDS EYE® Sweet Corn or Mixed Vegetables**
- ¹/₂ **teaspoon salt**
- ¹/₂ **teaspoon dried oregano leaves**
- ¹/₂ **teaspoon chili powder**
- ¹/₄ **teaspoon garlic powder**
- ¹/₈ **teaspoon pepper**
- 1¹/₂ **cups MINUTE® Rice**

Brown meat in large skillet. Add tomatoes, water, corn and seasonings. Bring to a boil and boil about 2 minutes. Stir in rice. Cover; remove from heat. Let stand 5 minutes. Fluff with a fork. Makes 4 servings.

QUICK AND EASY SPANISH RICE AND BEEF

SUKIYAKI

1 pound round steak, cut into thin strips
3 tablespoons butter or margarine
1 cup water
⅓ cup soy sauce
1½ cups sliced mushrooms*
1 can (8 oz.) bamboo shoots, drained*
½ cup celery strips*
1 medium red pepper, cut into thin strips*
4 scallions, cut into 1-inch pieces
1 beef bouillon cube
2 tablespoons sugar
1½ cups MINUTE® Rice

Brown beef in hot butter in large skillet. Add remaining ingredients, except rice. Bring to a full boil. Stir in rice. Cover; remove from heat. Let stand 5 minutes. Fluff with fork. Makes 4 servings.

*You may use 1 package (16 oz.) BIRDS EYE® FARM FRESH Broccoli, Red Peppers, Bamboo Shoots and Mushrooms for the mushrooms, bamboo shoots, celery and red pepper.

MIDDLE-EASTERN-STYLE BEEF

1 pound lean round steak, cut into thin strips
1 small onion, chopped
2 tablespoons butter or margarine
1 can (13¾ oz.) ready-to-serve beef broth
1½ cups BIRDS EYE® FARM FRESH Broccoli, Cauliflower and
      Carrots, thawed
¼ cup golden raisins
1 tablespoon lemon juice
¼ teaspoon salt
⅛ teaspoon ground cinnamon
1½ cups MINUTE® Rice
½ cup sliced almonds

Brown beef and onion in hot butter in large skillet. Add broth, vegetables, raisins, lemon juice, salt and cinnamon. Bring to a full boil. Stir in rice and almonds. Cover; remove from heat. Let stand 5 minutes. Fluff with fork. Makes 4 servings.

MANDARIN BEEF AND RICE

    3/4 **pound London broil, cut into thin strips**
      1 **tablespoon oil**
      1 **green pepper, cut into strips**
      2 **scallions, sliced**
      1 **garlic clove, minced**
      1 **can (11 oz.) mandarin orange sections**
    3/4 **cup water**
      2 **tablespoons soy sauce**
      2 **drops hot pepper sauce**
    1/2 **teaspoon salt**
   11/2 **cups MINUTE® Rice**

Brown beef in hot oil in large skillet. Add green pepper; cook and stir 3 minutes.
Add scallions and cook 1 to 2 minutes. Then add garlic and cook 15 seconds.
Add juice from orange sections, water, soy sauce, pepper sauce and salt. Bring
to a full boil. Stir in rice and oranges. Cover; remove from heat. Let stand 5
minutes. Fluff with fork. Makes 4 servings.

CANTONESE BEEF

1 pound round steak, cut into thin strips
2 tablespoons oil
1½ cups water
1 package mushroom gravy mix
1 red pepper, cut into thin strips
1 can (8 oz.) sliced water chestnuts, drained
4 scallions, sliced diagonally into 1-inch pieces
3 tablespoons soy sauce
1 teaspoon ground ginger
1½ cups MINUTE® Rice

Brown beef in hot oil in large skillet. Stir in water and gravy mix. Add red pepper, water chestnuts, scallions, soy sauce and ginger. Bring to a full boil. Stir in rice. Cover; remove from heat. Let stand 5 minutes. Fluff with fork. Makes 4 servings.

MICROWAVE DIRECTIONS: Mix all ingredients in 12×7½-inch microwavable dish. Cover with plastic wrap and cook at HIGH 4 minutes. Stir; cover and cook at HIGH 3 to 4 minutes longer. Let stand 5 minutes. Fluff with fork. Makes 4 servings.

CANTONESE BEEF

MEXICAN BEEF AND RICE

½ pound ground beef
4 scallions, thinly sliced*
1 can (8 oz.) tomato sauce
½ cup water
2 tablespoons sliced pitted ripe olives or stuffed green olives
1½ teaspoons chili powder
¾ cup MINUTE® Rice
Tortilla chips

Brown beef with scallions in large skillet, breaking beef into small pieces. Stir in tomato sauce, water, olives and chili powder. Bring to a full boil. Stir in rice. Cover; remove from heat. Let stand 5 minutes. Fluff with fork. Serve with tortilla chips. Makes 2 servings.

MICROWAVE DIRECTIONS: Place beef, in small pieces, and scallions in microwavable dish. Cover and cook at HIGH 2 minutes. Stir in remaining ingredients except tortilla chips. Cover and cook at HIGH 5 minutes longer. Let stand 5 minutes. Fluff with fork. Serve with tortilla chips. Makes 2 servings.

*You may use ½ cup chopped onion for the scallions.

Note: Recipe may be doubled, using range-top directions. Shredded cheddar cheese may be served with the tortilla chips.

MEXICAN BEEF AND RICE

STUFFED PEPPERS

6 medium green peppers*
Boiling salted water
1 pound ground beef
1 small onion, chopped
1 can (8 oz.) kidney beans, drained
1 can (8 oz.) tomato paste
2 1/2 cups water
1 1/2 teaspoons salt
1 teaspoon sugar
3/4 teaspoon chili powder
1/4 teaspoon garlic salt
1/3 cup shredded cheddar cheese (optional)
1 tablespoon butter or margarine (optional)
2 1/4 cups MINUTE® Rice

Cut slice from top of peppers; remove seeds. Cook, uncovered, in salted water to cover peppers about 5 minutes; drain.

Brown beef and onion in large skillet. Add beans, tomato paste, 1/4 cup of the water, 3/4 teaspoon of the salt, the sugar, chili powder and garlic salt; mix well. Spoon into peppers and place in 13×9-inch baking dish. Add small amount of water to cover bottom of dish. Bake at 375° for 25 minutes or until peppers are tender. Sprinkle with cheese.

Meanwhile, bring remaining 2 1/4 cups water, 3/4 teaspoon salt and the butter to a full boil in medium saucepan. Stir in rice. Cover; remove from heat. Let stand 5 minutes. Fluff with fork. Serve with peppers. Makes 6 servings.

HEARTY COUNTRY BEEF AND RICE

6 slices bacon, cut into 1-inch pieces
1 pound ground beef
1/2 cup chopped onion
2 cups (1/2 package) BIRDS EYE® FARM FRESH Broccoli,
    Corn and Red Peppers
1 can (10 3/4 oz.) condensed golden mushroom soup
1 cup water
1/4 teaspoon garlic powder
1 1/2 cups MINUTE® Rice

Cook bacon in large skillet until crisp. Remove bacon; drain on absorbent paper and set aside. Drain fat from skillet. Brown beef with onion in same skillet. Add vegetables, soup, water and garlic powder. Bring to a boil. Reduce heat; simmer 1 minute. Stir in rice. Cover; remove from heat. Let stand 5 minutes. Stir in bacon. Makes 4 servings.

Poultry Entrees

POLYNESIAN CHICKEN

2¹/₂ **pounds frying chicken pieces**
¹/₂ **cup seasoned all-purpose flour**
¹/₄ **cup butter or margarine**
1 **can (8¹/₄ oz.) pineapple chunks in syrup**
2 **tablespoons brown sugar**
1 **tablespoon vinegar**
1¹/₄ **cups water**
¹/₂ **teaspoon salt**
1¹/₂ **cups MINUTE® Rice**
1 **scallion, sliced**

Coat chicken with seasoned flour. Brown chicken well in hot butter in large skillet. Drain pineapple, reserving ¹/₄ cup syrup. Combine reserved syrup, brown sugar and vinegar in small bowl; pour over chicken. Turn chicken, skin side down. Reduce heat; cover and simmer until fork tender, about 20 minutes. Move chicken to side of skillet.

Add the pineapple, water and salt. Bring to a full boil. Stir in rice. Cover; remove from heat. Let stand 5 minutes. Fluff with fork. Garnish with scallion. Makes 4 servings.

Note: Flour may be seasoned with ¹/₄ teaspoon each pepper and ground nutmeg, or ¹/₂ teaspoon paprika and ¹/₄ teaspoon ground ginger.

POLYNESIAN CHICKEN

SOUTHERN-STYLE JAMBALAYA

- 1/2 **pound boned chicken breasts, cut into pieces**
- 2 **tablespoons butter or margarine**
- 12 **ounces Polish sausage (kielbasa), sliced**
- 1 **small green pepper, diced**
- 1 **small onion, diced**
- 1 **stalk celery, diced**
- 1 **can (14 1/2 oz.) stewed tomatoes**
- 1/2 **cup water**
- 1 1/2 **cups MINUTE® Rice**
- 1/2 **teaspoon salt**
- 1/2 **teaspoon hot pepper sauce**
- 1 **tablespoon chopped parsley (optional)**

Cook and stir chicken in hot butter in large skillet until lightly browned. Add sausage, green pepper, onion and celery; cook until vegetables are just tender, about 5 minutes. Mix in tomatoes and water; bring to a full boil. Stir in rice, salt and hot pepper sauce. Cover; remove from heat. Let stand 5 minutes. Fluff with fork; sprinkle with parsley. Makes 4 servings.

MICROWAVE DIRECTIONS: Combine chicken, butter, sausage, green pepper, onion and celery in 12×7 1/2-inch microwavable dish. Cover with plastic wrap and cook at HIGH 3 minutes; stir. Add tomatoes, water, rice, salt and hot pepper sauce. Cover and cook at HIGH 7 minutes longer. Let stand 5 minutes. Fluff with fork; sprinkle with parsley. Makes 4 servings.

SOUTHERN-STYLE JAMBALAYA

TURKEY RICE HASH

1 can (13³/₄ oz.) ready-to-serve chicken broth
2 medium onions, sliced
1 medium green pepper, diced
1 medium red pepper, diced
2 garlic cloves, minced
1 pound turkey breast or boned chicken breasts, cut into
   1-inch cubes
1 teaspoon dried thyme leaves
¼ teaspoon pepper
1½ cups MINUTE® Rice

Bring ¼ cup of the broth to a boil in large skillet with nonstick finish. Add onions, peppers and garlic and cook until crisp-tender. Add turkey and cook until opaque. Stir in thyme and pepper.

Add remaining broth and bring to a full boil. Stir in rice. Cover; remove from heat. Let stand 5 minutes. Fluff with fork. Makes 4 servings.

CHICKEN CONTINENTAL

6 ounces chicken, cut into strips
1 tablespoon oil
1 garlic clove, crushed
½ cup chicken broth
1 cup BIRDS EYE® Cut Green Beans, partially thawed
2 tablespoons canned sliced mushrooms, drained
½ teaspoon salt
¼ teaspoon dried tarragon leaves
   Dash of pepper
¾ cup MINUTE® Rice

Cook and stir chicken in hot oil in large skillet until lightly browned. Add garlic and cook until golden brown. Add broth, beans, mushrooms, salt, tarragon and pepper. Bring to a full boil. Stir in rice. Cover; remove from heat. Let stand 5 minutes. Fluff with fork. Makes 2 servings.

MICROWAVE DIRECTIONS: Combine chicken, oil and garlic in 1-quart microwavable dish. Stir to coat chicken with oil; cover. Cook at HIGH 5 minutes. Stir to separate chicken pieces. Add remaining ingredients. Cover and cook at HIGH 5 minutes longer. Let stand 5 minutes. Fluff with fork. Makes 2 servings.

CHICKEN CACCIATORE

1 pound boned chicken, cut into strips*
1/2 cup chopped onion
1 medium green pepper, cut into strips
1 garlic clove, minced
2 tablespoons butter or margarine
1 can (28 oz.) whole tomatoes
1 can (8 oz.) tomato sauce
1/2 teaspoon salt
1/2 teaspoon dried oregano leaves
1/2 teaspoon dried basil leaves
1/8 teaspoon ground red pepper (optional)
1 1/2 cups MINUTE® Rice

Cook and stir chicken with onion, green pepper and garlic in hot butter in large skillet until lightly browned. Add tomatoes, tomato sauce and seasonings. Bring to a full boil. Stir in rice. Cover; remove from heat. Let stand 5 minutes. Fluff with fork. Makes 4 servings.

MICROWAVE DIRECTIONS: Mix together chicken, onion, green pepper, garlic and butter in microwavable dish. Cover and cook at HIGH 5 minutes. Stir in remaining ingredients. Cover and cook at HIGH 5 to 6 minutes longer. Let stand 5 minutes. Fluff with fork. Makes 4 servings.

*You may use 1 pound cleaned shrimp for the chicken.

CLASSIC SAVORY CHICKEN DIVAN

3/4 pound boned chicken, cut into strips
2 teaspoons oil
1 cup water
1 tablespoon dry sherry
1 package (10 oz.) BIRDS EYE® Broccoli Spears or Deluxe
   Broccoli Florets
1 can (10 3/4 oz.) condensed cream of chicken soup
1 1/2 cups MINUTE® Rice
1 tablespoon grated Parmesan cheese

Cook and stir chicken in hot oil in large skillet until lightly browned. Add water, sherry, broccoli and soup. Bring to a full boil, separating broccoli spears. Stir in rice. Cover; remove from heat. Let stand 5 minutes. Arrange on platter. Sprinkle with cheese. Makes 4 servings.

MICROWAVE DIRECTIONS: Thaw broccoli, separating pieces. Place chicken and oil in 2-quart microwavable dish. Cook at HIGH 3 minutes, stirring once. Add water, sherry, broccoli, soup and rice. Cover and cook at HIGH 6 minutes longer. Let stand 5 minutes. Arrange on platter. Sprinkle with cheese. Makes 4 servings.

CHINESE-STYLE CHICKEN

1 pound boned chicken breasts, cut into strips
1 garlic clove, crushed
2 tablespoons oil
3 tablespoons soy sauce
1 tablespoon cornstarch
1 can (13¾ oz.) ready-to-serve chicken broth
2 large carrots, diagonally sliced into thin strips
1 cup snow pea pods*
1 can (14 oz.) baby cob corn, drained
2 scallions, diagonally sliced into ½-inch pieces
¾ to 1 teaspoon ground ginger
1½ cups MINUTE® Rice

Cook and stir chicken and garlic in hot oil in large skillet until chicken is lightly browned. Mix soy sauce and cornstarch in small cup; stir into chicken mixture. Add broth, vegetables and ginger. Cook and stir until mixture thickens and comes to a full boil. Stir in rice. Cover; remove from heat. Let stand 5 minutes. Fluff with fork. Garnish as desired. Makes 4 servings.

MICROWAVE DIRECTIONS: Omit oil. Spread chicken in single layer in microwavable dish. Cover and cook at HIGH 4 to 5 minutes. Mix soy sauce and cornstarch in small cup. Stir into chicken with remaining ingredients. Cover and cook at HIGH 5 minutes. Stir; cover and cook at HIGH 4 to 7 minutes longer or until thickened. Let stand 5 minutes. Fluff with fork. Makes 4 servings.

*You may use 1 cup broccoli florets for the snow pea pods.

CHINESE-STYLE CHICKEN

GINGER-SPICED CHICKEN

GINGER-SPICED CHICKEN

1¹/₃ cups water
2 teaspoons butter or margarine
¹/₂ teaspoon salt
1¹/₃ cups MINUTE® Rice
1 pound boned chicken breasts, cut into strips
2 garlic cloves, minced
2 tablespoons oil
1 large red pepper, cut into thin strips
1 large green pepper, cut into thin strips
1 cup sliced mushrooms
3 tablespoons soy sauce
1 tablespoon cornstarch
³/₄ cup water
¹/₂ teaspoon ground ginger
1 chicken bouillon cube
¹/₃ cup cashews or peanuts
1 tablespoon sesame seed (optional)

continued

Bring 1⅓ cups water, the butter and salt to a full boil. Stir in rice. Cover; remove from heat. Let stand 5 minutes. Meanwhile, cook and stir chicken and garlic in hot oil in large skillet until lightly browned. Stir in peppers and mushrooms. Cook and stir until crisp-tender, 2 to 3 minutes.

Mix soy sauce and cornstarch in cup; stir into chicken mixture. Add ¾ cup water, the ginger and bouillon cube. Cook and stir over medium heat until mixture thickens and comes to a boil. Cook 1 minute.

Spoon over rice and sprinkle with cashews and sesame seed. Makes 4 servings.

LEMON CHICKEN AND RICE

> **1 pound boned chicken breasts, cut into strips**
> **1 medium onion, chopped**
> **2 garlic cloves, crushed**
> **2 tablespoons butter or margarine**
> **1 can (13¾ oz.) ready-to-serve chicken broth**
> **1 tablespoon cornstarch**
> **1 large carrot, diagonally sliced**
> **2 tablespoons fresh lemon juice**
> **½ teaspoon grated lemon rind**
> **½ teaspoon salt**
> **1½ cups MINUTE® Rice**
> **1 cup snow pea pods or 1 package (6 oz.) frozen snow pea pods**
> **3 tablespoons chopped parsley**

Cook and stir chicken, onion and garlic in hot butter in large skillet until chicken is lightly browned. Mix broth and cornstarch in small bowl; stir into chicken mixture.

Add carrot, lemon juice, lemon rind and salt. Cook and stir until mixture thickens and comes to a full boil. Stir in rice, snow pea pods and parsley. Cover; remove from heat. Let stand 5 minutes. Fluff with fork. Makes 4 servings.

MICROWAVE DIRECTIONS: Reduce butter to 1 tablespoon. Combine chicken, onion, garlic and butter in 2½-quart microwavable dish. Cover and cook at HIGH 2 minutes. Stir; cover and cook at HIGH 1 to 2 minutes longer. Mix broth and cornstarch in small bowl; stir into chicken mixture. Add remaining ingredients. Cover and cook at HIGH 3 minutes. Stir; cover and cook at HIGH 3 minutes longer. Stir again; cover and cook at HIGH 1 minute or until thickened. Fluff with fork. Makes 4 servings.

CHICKEN AND HAM WITH RICE

³/₄ pound boned chicken breasts, cut into strips
4 ounces boiled ham, cut into strips
2 tablespoons butter or margarine
1 can (10³/₄ oz.) condensed cream of chicken soup
1 cup water
2 tablespoons Dijon-style mustard (optional)
1 package (10 oz.) BIRDS EYE® Asparagus Cuts, thawed
1¹/₂ cups MINUTE® Rice
2 slices Swiss cheese, cut into wedges or small cubes

Cook and stir chicken and ham in hot butter in large skillet until lightly browned.
Stir in soup, water and mustard; add asparagus. Bring to a full boil. Stir in rice
and top with cheese. Cover; remove from heat. Let stand 5 minutes. Fluff with
fork. Makes 4 servings.

MICROWAVE DIRECTIONS: Omit butter and increase water to 1³/₄ cups.
Combine chicken and ham in microwavable dish. Cover and cook at HIGH
4 minutes. Stir in remaining ingredients, except cheese. Cover and cook at HIGH
5 minutes. Stir again; cover and cook at HIGH 2 to 5 minutes. Top with cheese.
Cover and let stand 5 minutes. Fluff with fork. Makes 4 servings.

CHICKEN AND HAM WITH RICE

VEGETABLE-TURKEY ROLLS

- 1 cup water
- ½ teaspoon salt
- 1 package (16 oz.) BIRDS EYE® Broccoli Cuts
- 1 cup MINUTE® Rice
- 1 teaspoon butter or margarine
- 4 tablespoons prepared mustard
- 4 turkey cutlets, pounded
- ⅓ cup mayonnaise
- 2 tablespoons grated Parmesan cheese
- 2 tablespoons milk
- 1 teaspoon prepared mustard

Bring water, salt and broccoli cuts to a full boil in medium saucepan. Stir in rice and butter. Cover; remove from heat. Let stand 5 minutes. Fluff with fork.

Meanwhile, spread 1 tablespoon of the mustard onto each of the cutlets. Spoon about ⅓ cup of the vegetable-rice mixture onto the center of each cutlet. Roll up and place seam side down in 13×9-inch baking dish. Spoon remaining vegetable-rice mixture around the rolls in dish.

Mix mayonnaise, cheese, milk and the 1 teaspoon mustard in small bowl. Spoon over turkey rolls. Cover with foil and bake at 350° for 10 minutes. Uncover and bake 15 minutes longer. Makes 4 servings.

CHICKEN FLORENTINE

3/4 **pound boned chicken breasts, cut into strips**
1 **small onion, chopped**
2 **tablespoons butter or margarine**
1 **garlic clove, minced**
1 **package (10 oz.) BIRDS EYE® Chopped Spinach**
1 **cup chicken broth**
1/2 **cup water**
1 **cup MINUTE® Rice**
1/3 **cup grated Parmesan cheese**

Cook and stir chicken and onion in hot butter in large skillet until chicken is lightly browned. Add garlic and cook 30 seconds. Add spinach, broth and water. Bring to a boil. Reduce heat; simmer 3 minutes. Stir in rice and cheese. Cover; remove from heat. Let stand 5 minutes. Fluff with fork. Makes 3 servings.

MICROWAVE DIRECTIONS: Thaw and drain spinach, reduce broth to 3/4 cup and omit butter. Mix together chicken, onion and garlic in microwavable dish. Cover and cook at HIGH 3 minutes. Stir in spinach, broth, water and rice. Cover and cook at HIGH 6 minutes longer. Stir in cheese. Makes 3 servings.

CHICKEN AND PEACHES WITH SPICED RICE

2 **tablespoons all-purpose flour**
1/2 **teaspoon salt**
 Dash of pepper
2 **whole chicken breasts, split**
2 **tablespoons butter or margarine**
1 **small onion, chopped**
1 **can (16 oz.) sliced peaches in light syrup**
1 **cup chicken broth**
1 **tablespoon brown sugar**
1/2 **teaspoon ground cinnamon**
1/4 **teaspoon ground cloves**
2 **tablespoons lemon juice**
11/2 **cups MINUTE® Rice**

Mix flour, salt and pepper in shallow dish. Coat chicken with seasoned flour. Brown chicken in hot butter in large skillet. Stir in onion. Reduce heat to low. Cover and cook 20 minutes, or until chicken is fork tender. Remove chicken from skillet; set aside.

Drain peaches, pouring juice into skillet. Add broth, brown sugar, spices and lemon juice. Bring to a full boil. Stir in rice. Arrange chicken and peaches on top. Cover; remove from heat. Let stand 5 minutes. Makes 4 servings.

SWEET 'N SOUR CHICKEN

SWEET 'N SOUR CHICKEN

1 pound boned chicken, cut into cubes
2 tablespoons oil
1 cup green pepper strips
1 cup carrot strips
1 garlic clove, minced
1¼ cups chicken broth
1 can (8 oz.) pineapple chunks in juice
¼ cup soy sauce
3 tablespoons brown sugar
3 tablespoons vinegar
2 tablespoons dry sherry (optional)
½ teaspoon ground ginger
1½ cups MINUTE® Rice

Cook and stir chicken in hot oil in large skillet until well browned. Add green pepper, carrot and garlic and cook and stir 1 to 2 minutes.

Add broth, pineapple with juice, soy sauce, brown sugar, vinegar, sherry and ginger. Bring to a full boil. Stir in rice. Cover; remove from heat. Let stand 5 minutes. Fluff with fork. Makes 4 servings.

MICROWAVE DIRECTIONS: Omit oil and reduce broth to 1 cup. Mix chicken, carrots and garlic in 2-quart microwavable dish. Cover and cook at HIGH 3 minutes. Stir in remaining ingredients. Cover and cook at HIGH 5 to 6 minutes longer. Let stand 5 minutes. Fluff with fork. Makes 4 servings.

CHICKEN-RICE AMANDINE

3/4 **pound boned chicken breasts, cut into strips**
1 **tablespoon oil**
2 **cups water**
1 **tablespoon cornstarch**
2 **cups (1/2 package) BIRDS EYE® FARM FRESH Broccoli,**
    Green Beans, Pearl Onions and Red Peppers
1 **teaspoon salt**
1/4 **teaspoon pepper**
1/4 **teaspoon dried tarragon leaves**
1 **chicken bouillon cube**
1 1/2 **cups MINUTE® Rice**
3 **tablespoons sliced almonds**

Cook and stir chicken in hot oil in large skillet until lightly browned. Mix water and cornstarch in bowl; stir into chicken. Add vegetables, seasonings and bouillon cube. Cook and stir until mixture thickens and comes to a full boil. Stir in rice. Cover; remove from heat. Let stand 5 minutes. Fluff with fork and sprinkle with almonds. Makes 4 servings.

MICROWAVE DIRECTIONS: Omit oil. Spread chicken in single layer in microwavable dish. Cover and cook at HIGH 3 to 4 minutes. Mix water and cornstarch in bowl; stir into chicken. Add remaining ingredients, except almonds. Cover and cook at HIGH 3 minutes. Stir; cover and cook at HIGH 3 minutes longer. Stir again; cover and cook at HIGH 2 to 5 minutes. Let stand 5 minutes. Fluff with fork and sprinkle with almonds. Makes 4 servings.

CHICKEN A LA KING

1 **pound boned chicken breasts, cut into strips**
2 **tablespoons butter or margarine**
1 **jar (12 oz.) home-style chicken gravy**
1 **package (10 oz.) BIRDS EYE® Green Peas**
1 **cup milk**
1 **jar (4.5 oz.) sliced mushrooms, drained**
2 **tablespoons dry sherry (optional)**
1/2 **teaspoon salt**
1/8 **teaspoon pepper**
1 1/2 **cups MINUTE® Rice**
1 **jar (4 oz.) pimiento pieces**

Cook and stir chicken in hot butter in large skillet until lightly browned. Add gravy, peas, milk, mushrooms, sherry, salt and pepper. Bring to a boil. Reduce heat; cover and simmer 2 minutes. Bring back to a full boil. Stir in rice and pimiento. Cover; remove from heat. Let stand 5 minutes. Fluff with fork. Makes 4 servings.

CHICKEN-RICE AMANDINE

COUNTRY-STYLE TURKEY

 1 pound turkey or chicken, cut into strips
 1/2 cup chopped onion
 2 tablespoons butter or margarine
 2 cups milk
 1 package (10 oz.) BIRDS EYE® Mixed Vegetables
 1 teaspoon salt
 3/4 teaspoon poultry seasoning
 1 1/2 cups MINUTE® Rice

Cook and stir turkey and onion in hot butter in large skillet until lightly browned. Add milk, vegetables, salt and poultry seasoning. Bring to a full boil. Stir in rice. Cover; remove from heat. Let stand 5 minutes. Fluff with fork. Makes 4 servings.

MICROWAVE DIRECTIONS: Omit butter and reduce milk to 1 3/4 cups. Mix turkey and onion in 2 1/2-quart microwavable dish. Cover and cook at HIGH 3 minutes. Add remaining ingredients. Cover and cook at HIGH 7 minutes. Stir, cover and cook at HIGH 5 minutes longer or until liquid is absorbed. Fluff with fork. Makes 4 servings.

TURKEY-SPINACH BAKE

 2 cups water
 1 1/2 cups MINUTE® Rice
 1/2 cup chopped onion
 2 tablespoons butter or margarine
 1 package (10 oz.) BIRDS EYE® Chopped Spinach
 1 can (10 3/4 oz.) condensed cream of chicken soup
 3/4 cup mayonnaise
 1 teaspoon salt
 1/2 teaspoon curry powder
 2 tablespoons chopped pimiento
 3 cups diced cooked turkey or chicken
 1/4 cup shredded cheddar or grated Parmesan cheese

Bring 1 1/2 cups of the water to a full boil in medium saucepan. Stir in rice. Cover; remove from heat. Let stand 5 minutes. Fluff with fork.

Meanwhile, cook and stir onion in hot butter in another medium saucepan until tender but not browned. Add spinach and remaining 1/2 cup water. Bring to a full boil, separating spinach with fork. Reduce heat; cover and simmer 2 minutes.

Mix soup, mayonnaise, salt and curry in medium bowl. Add spinach mixture, pimiento and half of the soup mixture to the rice. Mix well and spoon into 9 x 9-inch baking dish. Arrange turkey on rice mixture. Mix cheese with remaining soup mixture. Pour over turkey. Cover with foil and bake at 350° for 25 minutes. Uncover and bake 5 to 10 minutes longer or until hot and bubbly. Makes 4 servings.

CANTONESE CHICKEN AND RICE

CANTONESE CHICKEN AND RICE

³/₄ **pound chicken, cut into strips**
2 **tablespoons oil**
1 **cup sliced celery**
1 **cup small carrots, sliced diagonally**
1 **medium onion, chopped**
1¹/₂ **cups chicken broth**
3 **tablespoons soy sauce**
1 **package (6 oz.) frozen snow pea pods (optional)**
¹/₂ **cup sliced water chestnuts**
¹/₂ **teaspoon ground ginger**
1¹/₂ **cups MINUTE® Rice**

Cook and stir chicken in hot oil in large skillet until lightly browned. Add celery, carrots and onion and cook about 5 minutes. Add broth, soy sauce, snow pea pods, water chestnuts and ginger. Bring to a full boil. Stir in rice. Cover; remove from heat. Let stand 5 minutes. Fluff with fork. Makes 4 servings.

MICROWAVE DIRECTIONS: Reduce oil to 1 tablespoon. Place chicken, oil, celery, carrots and onion in 2-quart microwavable dish. Cover and cook at HIGH 3 minutes, stirring once. Mix in remaining ingredients. Cover and cook at HIGH 6 minutes longer. Let stand 5 minutes. Fluff with fork. Makes 4 servings.

Seafood Entrees

CRAB AND RICE PRIMAVERA

1½ cups BIRDS EYE® FARM FRESH Broccoli, Green Beans,
   Pearl Onions and Red Peppers
¼ cup water
1⅓ cups milk
 1 pound imitation crabmeat or crabmeat
 2 tablespoons butter or margarine
 1 teaspoon garlic salt
¾ teaspoon dried basil leaves
1½ cups MINUTE® Rice
½ cup grated Parmesan cheese

Bring vegetables and water to a boil in medium saucepan, stirring occasionally.
Reduce heat; cover and simmer 3 minutes.

Add milk, imitation crabmeat, butter, garlic salt and basil. Bring to a full boil. Stir
in rice and cheese. Cover; remove from heat. Let stand 5 minutes. Fluff with
fork. Makes 4 servings.

CRAB AND RICE PRIMAVERA

SHRIMP SCAMPI

1 pound shrimp, cleaned
1 onion, chopped
4 to 6 garlic cloves, minced
2 tablespoons butter or margarine
1½ cups water
1 package chicken gravy mix
1 red pepper, chopped
1 tablespoon lemon juice
½ teaspoon salt
1½ cups MINUTE® Rice
¼ cup chopped parsley

Cook and stir shrimp, onion and garlic in hot butter in large skillet until shrimp turn pink. Mix water with gravy mix in small bowl. Add to shrimp mixture with red pepper, lemon juice and salt. Bring to a full boil. Stir in rice and parsley. Cover; remove from heat. Let stand 5 minutes. Fluff with fork. Makes 4 servings.

MICROWAVE DIRECTIONS: Combine onion, garlic and butter in 12×7½-inch microwavable dish. Cover with plastic wrap and cook at HIGH 2 minutes. Mix water with gravy mix in small bowl. Add to onion mixture with remaining ingredients, except parsley. Cover and cook at HIGH 4 minutes. Stir; cover and cook at HIGH 3 to 4 minutes longer. Let stand 5 minutes. Stir in parsley. Makes 4 servings.

FRUITED COD AND RICE PILAF

1 can (11 oz.) mandarin orange sections
 Chicken broth
1½ cups MINUTE® Rice
2 tablespoons butter or margarine
1 small green pepper, cut into 1-inch pieces
½ cup diagonally sliced scallions
1 tablespoon oil
1 pound cod fillet, cut into 1-inch pieces
½ teaspoon garlic powder
¼ teaspoon ground ginger
¼ teaspoon salt
½ teaspoon soy sauce

Drain oranges, reserving juice. Add broth to juice to make 1½ cups; set aside. Cook and stir rice in hot butter in large skillet until golden. Add green pepper, scallions and oil; cook 2 minutes longer. Add fish and reserved liquid; stir gently. Add seasonings and soy sauce. Bring to a full boil. Add reserved orange sections. Cover; remove from heat. Let stand 5 minutes. Fluff with fork. Sprinkle with additional scallions, if desired. Makes 4 servings.

SHRIMP SCAMPI

HAM AND SCALLOP DINNER

- ½ pound bay scallops
- 1 small green pepper, chopped
- 2 tablespoons butter or margarine
- ¼ pound boiled ham, diced
- 1¼ cups water
- ¼ cup dry white wine or water
- 1 envelope GOOD SEASONS® Lemon and Herbs Salad Dressing Mix
- 1½ cups MINUTE® Rice
- ⅓ cup diced roasted pepper or chopped pimiento
- 2 tablespoons chopped parsley (optional)

Cook scallops and green pepper in hot butter in large skillet until scallops are opaque; add ham. Add water, wine and salad dressing mix. Bring to a full boil. Stir in rice and roasted pepper. Cover; remove from heat. Let stand 5 minutes. Fluff with fork. Sprinkle with parsley. Makes 4 servings.

HAM AND SCALLOP DINNER

CREAMY BASILED FISH

1 package (16 oz.) frozen flounder fillets, slightly thawed
1 tablespoon butter or margarine
1/3 cup chopped onion
1/2 teaspoon salt
1/2 of 16 oz. package (8 oz.) BIRDS EYE® FARM FRESH
   Individual Broccoli Spears
1 1/2 cups chicken broth
1/2 cup heavy cream, half and half or light cream
1/2 teaspoon dried basil leaves
1 1/2 cups MINUTE® Rice
1 tablespoon chopped parsley

Carefully cut fish into 8 squares. Melt butter in large skillet; add onion and salt. Place broccoli on one side of skillet and fish on the other. Cover and simmer 8 minutes, turning fish and broccoli once after 4 minutes.

Add broth, heavy cream and basil. Bring to a full boil. Stir in rice and parsley. Cover; remove from heat. Let stand 5 minutes. Fluff with fork. Makes 4 servings.

MICROWAVE DIRECTIONS: Carefully cut fish into 8 squares. Place butter, onion, salt, broccoli and flounder in microwavable dish, placing broccoli on one side and fish on the other. Cover and cook at HIGH 5 minutes. Rearrange fish and broccoli, moving pieces in center to the edge of the dish. Cover and cook at HIGH 3 minutes longer. Add remaining ingredients. Cover and cook at HIGH 5 minutes, stirring after 3 minutes. Let stand 5 minutes. Fluff with fork. Makes 4 servings.

ASPARAGUS-STUFFED FILLETS

1 package (10 oz.) BIRDS EYE® Asparagus Spears, thawed
4 sole or flounder fillets (about 4 oz. each)
1/2 cup sliced almonds
1/2 cup chopped onion
1 garlic clove, minced
1/4 cup butter or margarine
1 can (13 3/4 oz.) ready-to-serve chicken broth
1/2 teaspoon salt
1/4 teaspoon pepper
1 1/2 cups MINUTE® Rice

Place three or four asparagus spears on each of the fillets; roll up. Lightly brown rolled fillets, seam side down, with almonds, onions and garlic in hot butter in large skillet. Turn fillets. Add broth, salt and pepper. Bring to a full boil. Stir in rice. Cover; remove from heat. Let stand 5 minutes. Fluff rice with fork. Makes 4 servings.

TUNA-RICE QUICHE

1 package (10 oz.) BIRDS EYE® CLASSICS, Broccoli with
   Cheese Sauce, thawed
1 cup MINUTE® Rice
1 can (6 1/2 oz.) water-packed tuna, undrained*
1/4 cup grated Parmesan cheese
1/2 teaspoon dried dill weed or 1 teaspoon chopped fresh dill
1/2 teaspoon salt
1/4 teaspoon pepper
3 eggs
1 1/4 cups milk or half and half

Mix vegetables, rice, tuna, 3 tablespoons of the Parmesan cheese and the seasonings in 10-inch pie plate or quiche dish. Mix together eggs and milk in small bowl; pour over vegetable mixture. Mix thoroughly. Sprinkle with remaining cheese. Bake at 350° for 30 minutes or until set.

MICROWAVE DIRECTIONS: Mix vegetables, rice, tuna, 3 tablespoons of the Parmesan cheese and the seasonings in 10-inch microwavable plate or quiche dish. Mix together eggs and milk in small bowl; pour over vegetable mixture. Mix thoroughly. Cover with waxed paper. Cook at MEDIUM-HIGH (70%) 10 minutes. Stir well. Sprinkle with remaining cheese. Cover and rotate plate half turn. Cook at MEDIUM-HIGH 10 minutes longer or until liquid is absorbed. Let stand 5 minutes. Makes 6 servings.

*You may use 6 ounces diced cooked chicken for the tuna.

KEDGEREE

1 cup chicken broth
1/2 teaspoon curry powder
1 cup MINUTE® Rice
4 hard-cooked eggs
1 can (7 3/4 oz.) salmon, drained and flaked
1/2 cup sour cream or plain yogurt

Combine broth and curry in medium saucepan. Bring to a full boil. Stir in rice. Cover; remove from heat. Let stand 5 minutes.

Coarsely chop 2 of the eggs and add to rice with salmon. Mix in sour cream. Cut remaining 2 eggs into wedges or slices and use for garnish. Makes 4 servings.

PAELLA OLÉ

- ½ **pound shrimp, cleaned**
- 2 **garlic cloves, crushed**
- 2 **tablespoons butter or margarine**
- 1¼ **cups chicken broth**
- 1 **tablespoon cornstarch**
- 1 **can (14½ oz.) stewed tomatoes**
- ½ **cup sliced pepperoni**
- 1 **package (10 oz.) BIRDS EYE® CLASSICS, Peas and Pearl Onions, thawed**
- ¼ **teaspoon ground red pepper**
- 1½ **cups MINUTE® Rice**
- ⅛ **teaspoon saffron (optional)**

Cook and stir shrimp and garlic in hot butter in large skillet until shrimp turn pink. Mix broth and cornstarch in small bowl; stir into shrimp. Add tomatoes, pepperoni, vegetables and red pepper. Cook and stir until mixture thickens and comes to a full boil. Stir in rice and saffron. Cover; remove from heat. Let stand 5 minutes. Fluff with fork. Makes 4 servings.

MICROWAVE DIRECTIONS: Reduce butter to 1 tablespoon. Cook garlic and butter in 2½-quart microwavable dish at HIGH 1 minute. Mix broth and cornstarch in small bowl; stir into garlic mixture. Add remaining ingredients. Cover and cook at HIGH 3 minutes. Stir; cover and cook at HIGH 3 minutes longer. Stir again; cover and cook at HIGH 2 to 4 minutes longer or until thickened. Fluff with fork. Makes 4 servings.

PAELLA OLÉ

QUICK AND EASY TUNA RICE WITH PEAS

1 package (10 oz.) BIRDS EYE® Green Peas
1¼ cups water
1 can (11 oz.) condensed cheddar cheese soup
1 can (12½ oz.) tuna, drained and flaked
1 chicken bouillon cube
1½ cups MINUTE® Rice

Bring peas, water, soup, tuna and bouillon cube to a full boil in medium saucepan. Stir in rice. Cover; remove from heat. Let stand 5 minutes. Fluff with fork. Makes 4 servings.

SEAFOOD ELEGANTE

1½ cups water
¼ cup mayonnaise
1 teaspoon grated lemon rind
½ teaspoon salt
½ teaspoon dried dill weed or 1 teaspoon chopped fresh dill
⅛ teaspoon pepper
1½ cups MINUTE® Rice
1 medium carrot, grated
1 small zucchini, grated
1 stalk celery, sliced
4 flounder or sole fillets (6 oz. each)
2 tablespoons lemon juice
2 tablespoons sliced almonds

Mix water, mayonnaise, rind and seasonings in 13×9-inch pan. Stir in rice and vegetables. Cover with fillets. Sprinkle with lemon juice and almonds. Cover and bake at 350° for 20 minutes or until fish begins to flake when tested with a fork.

MICROWAVE DIRECTIONS: Mix water, mayonnaise, rind and seasonings in 13×9-inch microwavable dish. Stir in rice and vegetables. Cover with fillets. Sprinkle with lemon juice and almonds. Cover with plastic wrap and cook at HIGH 6 to 8 minutes or until fish begins to flake when tested with a fork. Makes 4 servings.

QUICK AND EASY TUNA RICE WITH PEAS

SEAFOOD CACCIATORE

SEAFOOD CACCIATORE

1 pound shrimp, cleaned
1 small onion, chopped
2 garlic cloves, minced
2 tablespoons oil
1 can (14¹/₂ oz.) whole tomatoes in juice
1 can (8 oz.) tomato sauce
1¹/₂ cups water
1 medium green pepper, cut into thin strips
³/₄ teaspoon dried basil leaves
¹/₂ teaspoon dried oregano leaves
¹/₂ teaspoon salt
¹/₈ teaspoon ground red pepper
1 chicken bouillon cube
1¹/₂ cups MINUTE® Rice
8 clams, well scrubbed

continued

Cook and stir shrimp with onion and garlic in hot oil in large skillet until shrimp turn pink. Stir in tomatoes with juice, tomato sauce, water, green pepper, seasonings and bouillon cube. Bring to a full boil, breaking up tomatoes with spoon. Stir in rice. Cover; remove from heat. Let stand 5 minutes.

Meanwhile, place clams on rack in pan with water below rack. Bring to a boil. Cover and steam 5 to 10 minutes or until clams open. Discard any unopened clams. Fluff rice mixture with fork and serve topped with clams. Makes 4 servings.

MICROWAVE DIRECTIONS: Combine shrimp, onion, garlic and oil in microwavable dish. Cover and cook at HIGH 4 minutes. Stir in remaining ingredients, except clams. Break up tomatoes with spoon. Cover and cook at HIGH 7 to 8 minutes longer. Let stand 5 minutes.

Meanwhile, arrange clams in microwavable dish. Cover and cook at HIGH 5 to 7 minutes or until shells are open and meat is firm. Discard any unopened clams. Fluff rice mixture with fork and serve topped with clams. Makes 4 servings.

RICE-STUFFED FLOUNDER

> 1 cup grated carrot
> 2/3 cup MINUTE® Rice
> 1/2 cup heavy cream or milk
> 2 tablespoons chopped scallions
> 1/2 teaspoon salt
> 1/2 teaspoon finely chopped fresh ginger or 1/4 teaspoon
>   ground ginger
> Dash of pepper
> 4 flounder fillets (4 oz. each)
> 1 tablespoon butter or margarine

Mix carrot, rice, cream, scallions, salt, ginger and pepper in medium bowl. Spread evenly over fillets. Fold fillets in half and place in 8-inch square pan. Dot with butter. Bake at 325° for 20 minutes or until fish begins to flake when tested with a fork.

MICROWAVE DIRECTIONS: Omit butter. Mix carrot, rice, cream, scallions, salt, ginger and pepper. Spread evenly over fillets. Fold fillets in half and place in 8-inch square microwavable dish. Cover with plastic wrap and cook at HIGH 3 minutes. Rotate dish. Cook at HIGH 3 to 4 minutes longer or until fish begins to flake when tested with a fork. Let stand 5 minutes. Makes 4 servings.

Side Dishes

SUMMER SQUASH AND ZUCCHINI CASSEROLE

  2 medium yellow summer squash, diced
  1 medium zucchini, diced
  1 small onion, chopped
1½ cups shredded Monterey Jack cheese
  1 cup grated Parmesan cheese
1½ cups milk
  2 eggs, beaten
  1 cup MINUTE® Rice
 ½ teaspoon salt
 ½ teaspoon Italian seasoning
 ⅛ teaspoon pepper

Combine all ingredients in large bowl; mix well. Pour into greased 9-inch square baking dish. Bake at 375° for 35 minutes or until liquid is absorbed. Makes 6 servings.

MICROWAVE DIRECTIONS: Combine all ingredients in large bowl; mix well. Pour into greased 9-inch square microwavable dish. Cook at HIGH 20 minutes or until liquid is absorbed. Makes 6 servings.

TOP: HOME-STYLE CREAMED CORN CASSEROLE (PAGE 75)
BOTTOM: SUMMER SQUASH AND ZUCCHINI CASSEROLE

CLASSIC SPANISH RICE

- 1½ cups MINUTE® Rice
- 1 onion, cut into thin wedges
- 1 garlic clove, minced
- ¼ cup (½ stick) butter or margarine
- 1½ cups water
- 1 can (8 oz.) tomato sauce
- 1 small green pepper, diced
- 1 teaspoon salt
- ½ teaspoon prepared mustard (optional)
  Sliced stuffed green olives

Cook and stir rice, onion and garlic in hot butter in large skillet over medium heat, stirring frequently until mixture is lightly browned. Stir in remaining ingredients except olives. Bring to a full boil. Cover; remove from heat. Let stand 5 minutes. Fluff with fork. Garnish with olives. Serve with chicken or your favorite main dish. Makes 4 servings.

CLASSIC SPANISH RICE

HOME-STYLE CREAMED CORN CASSEROLE

2 cans (17 oz. each) cream-style corn
1 cup MINUTE® Rice
1 egg, slightly beaten
1/2 teaspoon salt
1/8 teaspoon pepper
1/8 teaspoon ground nutmeg

Combine all ingredients in large bowl; mix well. Pour into greased 9-inch square baking dish. Bake at 375° for 25 minutes or until liquid is absorbed. Garnish as desired. Makes 6 servings.

MICROWAVE DIRECTIONS: Combine all ingredients in large bowl; mix well. Pour into greased 9-inch square microwavable dish. Cover with plastic wrap and cook at HIGH 15 minutes or until liquid is absorbed. Garnish as desired. Makes 6 servings.

KANSAS CITY GREEN RICE

1/3 cup chopped scallions
2 garlic cloves, minced
2 tablespoons butter or margarine
2 cups chicken broth
1 package (10 oz.) BIRDS EYE® Chopped Spinach, thawed
    and drained
1 teaspoon salt
1/4 teaspoon pepper
1/4 teaspoon dried thyme leaves
1/4 teaspoon dried basil leaves
1 1/2 cups MINUTE® Rice

Cook and stir scallions and garlic in hot butter in large skillet until tender but not browned. Add broth, spinach, salt, pepper, thyme and basil. Bring to a full boil. Stir in rice. Cover; remove from heat. Let stand 5 minutes. Fluff with fork. Makes 9 servings.

CHINESE-STYLE RICE

1 egg, beaten
1 garlic clove, crushed
1 tablespoon oil
1 can (13³/4 oz.) ready-to-serve chicken broth
4 scallions, sliced diagonally
1 large carrot, thinly sliced diagonally
1 can (8 oz.) sliced water chestnuts, drained
2 to 3 tablespoons soy sauce
2 teaspoons brown sugar
1/2 teaspoon ground ginger
1¹/2 cups MINUTE® Rice

Cook and stir egg and garlic in hot oil in large skillet, stirring constantly to scramble egg and break into pieces. Add broth, scallions, carrot, water chestnuts, soy sauce, brown sugar and ginger. Bring to a full boil. Stir in rice. Cover; remove from heat. Let stand 5 minutes. Fluff with fork. Makes 4 servings.

BROCCOLI AND RICE WITH WALNUTS

1/4 cup coarsely chopped walnuts or slivered almonds
1 tablespoon oil
1/2 package (2¹/4 cups) BIRDS EYE® Broccoli Cuts*
2 tablespoons sliced scallions
1 garlic clove, minced
1 cup chicken broth or water
2 tablespoons dry sherry (optional)
1¹/2 tablespoons soy sauce
1 cup MINUTE® Rice

Cook and stir walnuts in hot oil in large skillet until lightly browned; remove from skillet. Add broccoli, scallions and garlic to oil remaining in skillet. Cook and stir 2 to 3 minutes. Add broth, sherry and soy sauce. Bring to a full boil. Stir in rice. Cover; remove from heat. Let stand 5 minutes. Fluff with fork and sprinkle with walnuts. Makes 4 servings.

*You may use 1 package (9 oz.) BIRDS EYE® Cut Green Beans for the broccoli.

PIZZA RICE

- 1 large green pepper, chopped
- 1 garlic clove, minced
- 2 tablespoons butter or margarine
- 1½ cups water
- 1 can (8¼ oz.) whole tomatoes
- 1 envelope GOOD SEASONS® Italian Salad Dressing Mix
- 1½ cups MINUTE® Rice
- 1 cup shredded mozzarella cheese
- ½ cup sliced pitted ripe olives
- 1 tablespoon grated Parmesan cheese (optional)

Cook and stir pepper and garlic in hot butter in large skillet until tender. Add water and tomatoes, breaking up tomatoes with spoon. Stir in salad dressing mix. Bring to a full boil. Stir in rice, ¾ cup of the mozzarella cheese and the olives. Cover; remove from heat. Let stand 5 minutes. Fluff with fork. Sprinkle with remaining mozzarella cheese and the Parmesan cheese. Serve with hamburgers, tomato slices, onion rings and lettuce or your favorite main dish. Makes 4 servings.

MICROWAVE DIRECTIONS: Combine all ingredients except cheeses and olives in microwavable bowl. Cover with plastic wrap and cook at HIGH 4 minutes. Stir; cover and cook at HIGH 3 to 5 minutes longer. Let stand 5 minutes. Stir in ¾ cup of the mozzarella cheese and the olives. Sprinkle with remaining mozzarella cheese and the Parmesan cheese. Serve with hamburgers, tomato slices, onion rings and lettuce or your favorite main dish. Makes 4 servings.

QUICK AND EASY ONION RICE

**1 can (10½ oz.) condensed onion soup or 1 envelope
instant onion soup mix**
1½ cups water
1 tablespoon butter or margarine
½ teaspoon salt
1½ cups MINUTE® Rice
Chopped parsley (optional)

Combine soup, water, butter and salt in medium saucepan. Bring to a full boil.
Stir in rice. Cover; remove from heat. Let stand 10 minutes. Fluff with fork.
Sprinkle with parsley. Serve with stew or your favorite main dish. Makes 4
servings.

SAVORY LEMON RICE

½ garlic clove, minced
2 tablespoons butter, margarine or oil
1½ cups chicken broth
½ teaspoon salt
1½ cups MINUTE® Rice
2 tablespoons chopped parsley
1 tablespoon lemon juice
1 teaspoon shredded lemon rind

Cook and stir garlic in hot butter in medium saucepan until lightly browned. Add
broth and salt. Bring to a full boil. Stir in rice. Cover; remove from heat. Let
stand 5 minutes. Stir in parsley, lemon juice and rind. Serve with shrimp or your
favorite main dish. Garnish as desired. Makes 4 servings.

MICROWAVE DIRECTIONS: Combine garlic, butter, broth, salt and rice in
microwavable bowl. Cover with plastic wrap and cook at HIGH 4 minutes. Stir;
cover and cook at HIGH 3 to 5 minutes longer. Let stand 5 minutes. Stir in
parsley, lemon juice and rind. Serve with shrimp or your favorite main dish.
Garnish as desired. Makes 4 servings.

QUICK AND EASY ONION RICE

CARROTS IN ORANGE RICE

1¹/₂ cups sliced carrots
¹/₃ cup orange juice
¹/₃ cup raisins (optional)
1 cup MINUTE® Rice
¹/₂ teaspoon grated orange rind

Cook carrots in medium saucepan with water to cover until tender, about 10 minutes. Drain, reserving ³/₄ cup liquid. Combine measured liquid, orange juice and raisins in medium saucepan. Bring to a full boil. Stir in rice and orange rind. Cover; remove from heat. Let stand 5 minutes. Stir in carrots. Makes 4 servings.

LOUISIANA CAJUN RICE

1 medium onion, chopped
2 tablespoons oil
1 can (13³/₄ oz.) ready-to-serve chicken broth
1 large red, green or yellow pepper, or a combination, sliced into thin strips
1¹/₂ to 2 teaspoons chili powder
¹/₂ teaspoon dried thyme leaves
¹/₄ teaspoon paprika
¹/₈ to ¹/₄ teaspoon ground red pepper
1¹/₂ cups MINUTE® Rice

Cook and stir onion in hot oil in medium saucepan until tender but not browned. Add broth, pepper strips and seasonings. Bring to a full boil. Stir in rice. Cover; remove from heat. Let stand 5 minutes. Fluff with fork. Makes 4 servings.

RISOTTO MILANESE

2 tablespoons butter or margarine
¹/₄ cup chopped onion
1 can (10³/₄ oz.) condensed chicken broth
¹/₄ cup white wine
¹/₄ teaspoon salt
¹/₈ teaspoon saffron (optional)
1¹/₂ cups MINUTE® Rice
1 tablespoon grated Parmesan cheese

Melt 1 tablespoon of the butter in medium saucepan. Cook and stir onion in hot butter until tender but not browned. Add broth, wine, salt and saffron. Bring to a full boil. Stir in rice. Cover; remove from heat. Let stand for 5 minutes. Stir in remaining 1 tablespoon butter and the cheese. Makes 4 servings.

SAUCY PEAS AND RICE

- **1 cup sliced mushrooms**
- **1 tablespoon butter or margarine**
- **1 package (10 oz.) BIRDS EYE® Green Peas**
- **1 can (10³/₄ oz.) condensed cream of mushroom soup**
- **1 cup milk**
- **Dash of pepper**
- **1¹/₂ cups MINUTE® Rice**

Cook and stir mushrooms in hot butter in large skillet until lightly browned. Add peas, soup, milk and pepper. Bring to a boil. Reduce heat; cover and simmer 2 minutes. Stir in rice. Cover; remove from heat. Let stand 5 minutes. Fluff with fork. Serve with lamb chops or your favorite main dish. Makes 4 servings.

MICROWAVE DIRECTIONS: Mix ingredients in microwavable dish. Cover and cook at HIGH 3 minutes. Stir; cover and cook at HIGH 6 minutes longer. Fluff with fork. Serve with lamb chops or your favorite main dish. Makes 4 servings.

SAUCY PEAS AND RICE

SHERRIED MUSHROOM RICE

SHERRIED MUSHROOM RICE

    1 garlic clove, minced
    2 tablespoons butter or margarine
    2 cups sliced mushrooms
  1/4 cup chopped red pepper
1 1/4 cups chicken broth
  1/4 cup dry sherry or chicken broth
    2 teaspoons onion flakes
  1/2 teaspoon salt
1 1/2 cups MINUTE® Rice
    2 tablespoons grated Parmesan cheese
    1 tablespoon chopped parsley

Cook and stir garlic in hot butter in large skillet 1 minute. Add mushrooms and red pepper; cook, stirring occasionally, 2 minutes.

Add broth, sherry, onion flakes and salt. Bring to a full boil. Stir in rice. Cover; remove from heat. Let stand 5 minutes. Fluff with fork and sprinkle with grated cheese and parsley. Serve with steak or your favorite main dish. Garnish as desired. Makes 4 servings.

MICROWAVE DIRECTIONS: Cut butter into pieces. Cook garlic, butter and mushrooms in microwavable dish at HIGH 2 to 3 minutes. Stir in remaining ingredients except Parmesan cheese and parsley. Cover and cook at HIGH 4 minutes. Stir; cover and cook at HIGH 2 to 3 minutes longer. Let stand 5 minutes. Fluff with fork and sprinkle with Parmesan cheese and parsley. Serve with steak or your favorite main dish. Makes 4 servings.

FESTIVE RICE

2¼ cups MINUTE® Rice
1 medium green pepper, chopped*
¼ cup oil
1 envelope GOOD SEASONS® Italian or Mild Italian Salad
   Dressing Mix
2¼ cups water
2 tablespoons chopped pimiento or parsley

Cook and stir rice and green pepper in hot oil in large skillet about 2 minutes. Sprinkle with salad dressing mix. Stir in water. Cover and bring to a boil. Remove from heat. Let stand 5 minutes. Stir in pimiento. Makes 6 servings.

*You may use ½ medium green pepper, chopped, and ½ cup grated carrot for the green pepper.

FRESH VEGETABLE RICE

1 large sweet onion, sliced into thin rings
1 large carrot, sliced diagonally
1 stalk celery, sliced diagonally
2 tablespoons butter or margarine
1 can (13¾ oz.) ready-to-serve chicken broth
¼ teaspoon dried thyme leaves
1½ cups MINUTE® Rice

Cook and stir onion, carrot and celery in hot butter in large skillet until tender but not browned. Add broth and thyme. Bring to a full boil. Stir in rice. Cover; remove from heat. Let stand 5 minutes. Fluff with fork. Serve with pork chops or your favorite main dish. Makes 4 servings.

CRANBERRY-APPLE RICE

1 cup water
1 cup cranberry sauce or cranberry-orange sauce
1 apple, peeled and diced or sliced
1 tablespoon butter or margarine
½ teaspoon salt
   Dash of ground cinnamon (optional)
1½ cups MINUTE® Rice

Combine water, cranberry sauce, apple, butter, salt and cinnamon in medium saucepan. Bring to a full boil. Stir in rice. Cover; remove from heat. Let stand 5 minutes. Fluff with fork. Makes 4 servings.

EASY MIDEASTERN PILAF

1¹/₂ cups beef broth
1 medium onion, chopped
¹/₄ cup raisins
2 tablespoons butter or margarine
¹/₄ teaspoon salt
1¹/₂ cups MINUTE® Rice
¹/₂ cup sliced almonds
2 tablespoons chopped parsley

Combine broth, onion, raisins, butter and salt in medium saucepan. Bring to a full boil. Stir in rice. Cover; remove from heat. Let stand 5 minutes. Stir in almonds and parsley. Serve with kabobs or your favorite main dish. Makes 4 servings.

MICROWAVE DIRECTIONS: Combine all ingredients except almonds and parsley in microwavable bowl. Cover with plastic wrap and cook at HIGH 4 minutes. Stir; cover and cook at HIGH 3 to 4 minutes longer. Let stand 5 minutes. Stir in almonds and parsley. Serve with kabobs or your favorite main dish. Makes 4 servings.

RICE STUFFING

1 cup chopped celery with leaves
¹/₂ cup chopped onion
3 tablespoons butter or margarine
1¹/₂ cups water
1 teaspoon salt
¹/₄ teaspoon poultry seasoning
¹/₈ teaspoon pepper
1¹/₂ cups MINUTE® Rice

Cook and stir celery with onion in hot butter in large skillet over medium-high heat until tender but not browned. Add water and seasonings. Bring to a full boil. Stir in rice. Cover; remove from heat. Let stand 5 minutes. Fluff with fork.

Stuffing may also be spooned lightly into chicken or other poultry, or use boneless veal or pork roasts. Do not pack tightly. Roast at once. Makes about 4 cups or enough to stuff a 3- to 4-pound chicken.

EASY MIDEASTERN PILAF

GARDEN MEDLEY RICE

GARDEN MEDLEY RICE

1 can (13³/₄ oz.) ready-to-serve chicken broth
2 cups assorted vegetables (broccoli florets, sliced yellow
    squash, peas, grated carrot)
1 teaspoon onion flakes
2 teaspoons snipped fresh rosemary or 1 teaspoon dried
    rosemary leaves
¹/₄ teaspoon garlic powder
1¹/₂ cups MINUTE® Rice
    Freshly ground pepper (optional)

Stir together broth, vegetables, onion flakes, rosemary and garlic powder in saucepan and bring to a full boil. Stir in rice. Cover; remove from heat. Let stand 5 minutes. Fluff with fork and sprinkle with pepper. Serve with chicken cutlets or your favorite main dish. Makes 4 servings.

MICROWAVE DIRECTIONS: Stir together all ingredients except pepper in microwavable bowl. Cover with plastic wrap and cook at HIGH 4 minutes. Stir; cover and cook at HIGH 3 to 5 minutes longer. Stir again; cover and cook at HIGH 3 minutes. Let stand 5 minutes. Fluff with fork and sprinkle with pepper. Serve with chicken cutlets or your favorite main dish. Makes 4 servings.

TEX-MEX RICE AND BEANS

- 1/2 cup chopped onion
- 1 garlic clove, minced
- 1 tablespoon oil
- 1 can (15 oz.) red kidney beans, drained
- 1 can (10 1/2 oz.) condensed beef bouillon
- 1 medium green pepper, diced
- 1/2 cup barbecue sauce
- 1 1/2 cups MINUTE® Rice

Cook and stir onion and garlic in hot oil in large skillet until onion is tender but not browned. Stir in beans, bouillon, green pepper and barbecue sauce. Bring to a full boil. Stir in rice. Cover; remove from heat. Let stand 5 minutes. Fluff with fork. Makes 4 servings.

MICROWAVE DIRECTIONS: Omit oil. Mix all ingredients in microwavable dish. Cover and cook at HIGH 5 minutes. Stir; cover and cook at HIGH 3 minutes longer. Stir; cover and let stand 5 minutes. Makes 4 servings.

CREAMY ALMOND RICE

- 1 small onion, chopped
- 1 tablespoon butter or margarine
- 1 can (13 3/4 oz.) ready-to-serve chicken broth
- 1/2 teaspoon salt
- 1/8 teaspoon pepper
- 1 1/2 cups MINUTE® Rice
- 1/2 small red pepper, cut into thin strips
- 2 tablespoons chopped parsley
- 1/2 cup sour cream
- 1/4 cup toasted slivered almonds

Cook and stir onion in hot butter in large skillet until tender but not browned. Add broth, salt and pepper. Bring to a full boil. Stir in rice, red pepper and parsley. Cover; remove from heat. Let stand 5 minutes. Fluff with fork and stir in sour cream and almonds. Makes 4 servings.

Desserts

OLD-FASHIONED RICE PUDDING

> 4 cups cold milk
> 1 cup MINUTE® Rice
> 1 package (4-serving size) JELL-O® Vanilla or Coconut
>   Cream Flavor Pudding and Pie Filling
> 1/4 cup raisins (optional)
> 1 egg, well beaten
> 1/4 teaspoon ground cinnamon
> 1/8 teaspoon ground nutmeg

Combine milk, rice, pudding mix, raisins and egg in medium saucepan. Bring to a full boil over medium heat, stirring constantly. Remove from heat. Cool 5 minutes, stirring twice. Pour into individual dessert dishes or serving bowl. Sprinkle with cinnamon and nutmeg; serve warm. (For chilled pudding, place plastic wrap directly on hot pudding. Cool slightly; then chill about 1 hour. Stir before serving; sprinkle with cinnamon and nutmeg.) Makes 10 servings.

Old-Fashioned Fruited Rice Pudding: Add 1 can (17½ oz.) drained fruit cocktail to pudding after cooling 5 minutes. Garnish as desired.

CREAMY LOW-CALORIE RICE PUDDING

> 1 package (4-serving size) JELL-O® Sugar Free Vanilla
>   Pudding and Pie Filling
> 3 cups skim or low-fat milk
> 1/2 cup MINUTE® Rice
> 1/4 cup raisins
> 1/8 teaspoon ground cinnamon

Combine all ingredients in medium saucepan. Bring to a boil over medium heat, stirring constantly. Pour into 1-quart casserole or individual dessert dishes. Place plastic wrap directly on surface of hot pudding. Chill 30 minutes; remove plastic wrap. Sprinkle with additional cinnamon, if desired. Makes 8 servings.

TOP: OLD-FASHIONED FRUITED RICE PUDDING
BOTTOM: OLD-FASHIONED RICE PUDDING

MAPLE RICE FLAN

MAPLE RICE FLAN

3 cups milk
³/₄ cup MINUTE® Rice
1 package (3 oz.) JELL-O® AMERICANA® Golden Egg
   Custard Mix
1 egg yolk
2 tablespoons sugar
¹/₄ teaspoon ground nutmeg
6 tablespoons LOG CABIN® Syrup

Combine milk, rice, custard mix, egg yolk, sugar and nutmeg in medium saucepan. Bring to a full boil over medium heat, stirring constantly. Cover; remove from heat. Let stand 5 minutes.

Meanwhile, pour 1 tablespoon syrup into each of 6 custard cups. Pour custard over syrup. Cover and chill until set. Just before serving, invert cups and unmold onto dessert plates. Makes 6 servings.

MICROWAVE RICE PUDDING

3¼ **cups milk**
¾ **cup MINUTE® Rice**
1 **package (4-serving size) JELL-O® French Vanilla Flavor**
  Pudding and Pie Filling
¼ **teaspoon ground cinnamon**
⅛ **teaspoon ground nutmeg**
2 **teaspoons grated orange rind (optional)**
⅓ **cup raisins**
1 **tablespoon butter or margarine**

MICROWAVE DIRECTIONS: Mix together all ingredients in 2-quart microwavable bowl. Cook, uncovered, at HIGH 3 minutes. Stir and cook at HIGH 2 minutes longer. Stir again and cook at HIGH 3 to 4 minutes or until mixture comes to a boil. Place plastic wrap directly on surface of hot pudding. Cool 15 minutes at room temperature or in refrigerator. Stir before serving. Serve warm or chilled. Makes 7 servings.

RICE PEACH MELBA

¾ **cup MINUTE® Rice**
1¾ **cups milk**
¼ **cup sugar**
½ **teaspoon salt**
⅛ **teaspoon ground nutmeg**
1 **cup thawed BIRDS EYE® COOL WHIP® Non-Dairy Whipped**
  Topping
6 **drained canned peach halves**
2 **tablespoons currant jelly or raspberry preserves, melted**

Mix rice and milk in medium saucepan. Bring to a boil. Reduce heat; simmer gently, covered, 15 minutes, fluffing rice occasionally with fork. Remove from heat. Stir in sugar, salt and nutmeg. Cool 5 minutes; then cover and chill about 1 hour.

Fold in whipped topping and spoon into serving bowl or dessert dishes. Arrange peach halves on top. Spoon melted jelly over the peaches. Makes 6 servings.

CHOCOLATE-COCONUT RICE SQUARES

1½ cups water
¼ cup sugar
½ teaspoon salt
1½ cups MINUTE® Rice
1 cup BAKER'S® Real Semi-Sweet Chocolate Chips
½ cup BAKER'S® ANGEL FLAKE® Coconut
1 cup thawed BIRDS EYE® COOL WHIP® Non-Dairy Whipped
       Topping

Combine water, sugar and salt in medium saucepan. Bring to a full boil. Stir in rice. Cover; remove from heat. Let stand 5 minutes. Add chips and coconut to hot rice and stir until chips are melted. Cover and chill.

Fold whipped topping into rice mixture. Pour into waxed paper-lined 8-inch square pan or 9×5-inch loaf pan. Cover and chill until firm, about 1 hour.

Invert onto serving plate and remove paper. Cut into squares or slices. Makes 6 servings.

GLORIFIED RICE

½ cup water
1 teaspoon butter or margarine
¼ teaspoon salt
½ cup MINUTE® Rice
1 can (8 oz.) crushed pineapple in juice, well drained
1 cup BAKER'S® ANGEL FLAKE® Coconut
1 cup miniature marshmallows
¼ cup chopped drained maraschino cherries
1¾ cups (4 oz.) BIRDS EYE® COOL WHIP® Non-Dairy Whipped
       Topping, thawed
3 tablespoons milk

Combine water, butter and salt in medium saucepan. Bring to a full boil. Stir in rice. Cover; remove from heat. Let stand 5 minutes. Fluff with fork. Cool.

Stir in pineapple, coconut, marshmallows and cherries. Fold in whipped topping and milk. Cover and chill about 1 hour. Garnish as desired. Makes 8 servings.

TOP: CHOCOLATE-COCONUT RICE SQUARES
BOTTOM: GLORIFIED RICE

Index